DEVELO
RATIONAL ~~EMOTIVE~~
BEHAVIOURAL
COUNSELLING

Developing Counselling, edited by Windy Dryden, is an innovative series of books which provides counsellors and counselling trainees with practical hints and guidelines on the problems they face in the counselling process. The books assume that readers have a working knowledge of the approach in question, and, in a clear and accessible fashion show how the counsellor can more effectively translate that knowledge into everyday practice.

Books in the series include:

Developing the Practice of Counselling
Windy Dryden and Colin Feltham

Developing Counsellor Supervision
Colin Feltham and Windy Dryden

Developing Counsellor Training
Windy Dryden and Colin Feltham

Developing Person-Centred Counselling
Dave Mearns

Developing Psychodynamic Counselling
Brendan McLoughlin

Developing Cognitive-Behavioural Counselling
Michael J. Scott, Stephen G. Stradling and Windy Dryden

DEVELOPING RATIONAL EMOTIVE BEHAVIOURAL COUNSELLING

Windy Dryden and
Joseph Yankura

SAGE Publications
London • Thousand Oaks • New Delhi

SAGE Publications Ltd
6 Bonhill Street
London EC2A 4PU

SAGE Publications Inc
2455 Teller Road
Newbury Park, California 91320

SAGE Publications India Pvt Ltd
32, M-Block Market
Greater Kailash – I
New Delhi 110 048

British Library Cataloguing in Publication data

A catalogue record for this book is
available from the British Library.

ISBN 0 8039 7754 9
ISBN 0 8039 7755 7 pbk

Library of Congress catalog record available

Typeset by Mayhew Typesetting, Rhayader, Powys
Printed in Great Britain by Biddles Ltd, Guildford, Surrey

Contents

Introduction

In this Introduction we will cover the basic principles of rational emotive behavioural counselling (REBC). Specifically, we will consider

1 REBC's specific principle of emotional responsibility;
2 the two types of psychological disturbance;
3 the REBC model of healthy and unhealthy negative emotions;
4 the principle of psychological interactionism;
5 the process of therapeutic change.

We will also introduce the now famous 'ABCDE' of REBC.

REBC's specific principle of emotional responsibility

Epictetus, the famous Roman philosopher, once said that people are disturbed not by events, but by the views they take of these events. This statement is at the heart of the cognitive theory of emotional disturbance, but is too vague for REBC. The specific principle of emotional responsibility that is at the heart of REBC is so termed because it specifies precisely the kinds of 'views' that are at the core of psychological disturbance and, as importantly, the kinds of 'views' that are at the core of psychological well-being. In outlining the REBC position on this issue, we will present four belief pairs. The first belief in the pair will be that associated with psychological health and the second that associated with psychological disturbance. In the language of REBC, the first are known as rational beliefs and the second, irrational beliefs. Before we present the four belief pairs that describe precisely how we disturb ourselves about self, others and life conditions and what we would have to think to be healthy instead, let us briefly discuss the terms 'rational' and 'irrational' as they are used in REBC theory.

Rational and irrational

The term 'rational' in REBC theory refers to beliefs which are

1 flexible;

2   consistent with reality;
3   logical; and which
4   promote the person's psychological well-being and aid her pursuit of her personally meaningful goals.

In contrast, the term 'irrational' in REBC theory refers to beliefs which are

1   rigid;
2   inconsistent with reality;
3   illogical; and which
4   interfere with the person's psychological well-being and get in the way of her pursuing her personally meaningful goals.

The four belief pairs

Preferences vs musts   Rational beliefs are flexible in nature and are often couched in the form of preferences (or its synonyms, for example, wishes, wants, desires etc.). Preferences can point to what we want to happen (for example, 'I want to pass my driving test') or to what we do not want to occur (for example, 'I don't want to get into trouble with my boss'). However, to understand the full meaning of a preference, its non-dogmatic nature needs to be made explicit in the person's statement. To take the two examples that we have just mentioned, we can tell that they are really preferences thus:

'I want to pass my driving test, BUT I don't have to do so.'

'I don't want to get into trouble with my boss, BUT there's no reason why I must not do so.'

The reason why it is so important for a preference to be phrased in its full form is that if it is expressed in its partial form ('I want to pass my driving test'), then it is easy for us to change it implicitly to a dogmatic must ('I want to pass my driving test (and therefore I have to do so)'). Indeed, the stronger our preferences, the more likely we are, if left to our own devices, to change these preferences into musts.

Preferences are rational because they are

1   flexible (that is, they allow for what is not preferred to occur);
2   consistent with reality (that is, they are consistent with the inner reality of the person's preferences);
3   logical; and they
4   promote the person's psychological well-being and aid her

pursuit of her personally meaningful goals (that is, they lead to healthy negative emotions when the person's preferences are not met which in turn facilitate effective problem-solving or constructive adjustment if changes cannot be made).

Irrational beliefs are rigid in nature and are often couched in the form of musts (or its synonyms, such as absolute shoulds, have to's, got to's etc.). Musts indicate that we believe that what we want absolutely *has to* occur ('I absolutely have to pass my driving test') or that what we do not want absolutely *should not* happen ('I must not get into trouble with my boss').

Musts are irrational because they are:

1   inflexible (that is, they do not allow for what must happen not to occur);
2   inconsistent with reality (that is, if there was a law of the universe that says I must pass my driving test, I could not possibly fail – this law, of course, does not exist);
3   illogical (that is, they do not logically follow on from the person's preferences); and they
4   interfere with the person's psychological well-being and get in the way of her pursuing her personally meaningful goals (that is, they lead to unhealthy negative emotions when the person's demands are not met which in turn impede effective problem-solving or constructive adjustment if changes cannot be made).

Albert Ellis (1994), the founder of REBC, holds that non-dogmatic preferences are at the very core of psychological health and that three other major rational beliefs are derived from these preferences. Similarly, Ellis believes that dogmatic musts are at the very core of emotional disturbance and that three other irrational beliefs are derived from these musts.

Anti-awfulizing vs awfulizing   Anti-awfulizing beliefs are rational in the sense that they are first and foremost non-dogmatic. These beliefs, which in their full form are expressed thus: 'It would be very bad if I failed my driving test, but it wouldn't be awful', are flexibly located on a continuum ranging from 0 to 99.9 per cent badness. The stronger a person's unmet preference, the higher her evaluation will be placed on this continuum. However, an anti-awfulizing belief cannot reach 100 per cent, since as Smokey Robinson's mother used to tell her young son: 'From the time you are born 'till you ride in the hearse, there's nothing so bad that it couldn't be worse.' In this sense, an anti-awfulizing belief is consistent with reality. This belief is also logical since it makes sense in the context of the person's preference. Finally, it is constructive since it will help the person take effective action if the negative event that the person is facing can be changed and it will aid the person to make a healthy adjustment if the situation cannot be changed.

Awfulizing beliefs, on the other hand, are irrational in the sense that they are first and foremost dogmatic. They are rigidly located on a magical 'horror' continuum ranging from 101 per cent badness to infinity. They are couched in such statements as 'It's horrible that. . .', 'It's terrible that. . .', 'It's awful that. . .' and 'It's the end of the world that. . .'. When a person is awfulizing, she literally believes at the moment that nothing could be worse. In this sense, an awfulizing belief is inconsistent with reality. This belief is also illogical since it is a nonsensical conclusion from the person's implicit rational belief (for example, 'Because it would be very bad if I failed my driving test it would therefore be awful if this happened'). Finally, it is unconstructive since it will interfere with the person taking effective action if the negative event that the person is facing can be changed and it will stop the person making a healthy adjustment if the situation cannot be changed.

High frustration tolerance (HFT) vs low frustration tolerance (LFT)
High frustration tolerance beliefs are rational in the sense that they are again primarily flexible and not grossly exaggerated. These beliefs are expressed in their full form, thus: 'Failing my driving test would be difficult to tolerate, but I could stand it'. The stronger a person's unmet preference, the more difficult it would be for her to tolerate this situation, but if she holds an HFT belief, it would still be tolerable. In this sense, an HFT belief is consistent with reality. It is also logical since it again makes sense in the context of the person's preference. Finally, like a preference and an anti-awfulizing belief, it is constructive since it will help the person take effective action if the negative event that the person is facing can be changed and it will aid the person to make a healthy adjustment if the situation cannot be changed.

Low frustration tolerance beliefs, on the other hand, are irrational in the sense that they are first and foremost grossly exaggerated. They are couched in such statements as 'I can't stand it. . .', 'I can't bear it. . .', 'It's intolerable. . .'. When a person has a low frustration tolerance belief, she means one of two things:

1 she will disintegrate; or
2 she will never experience any happiness again.

Since these two statements are obviously untrue, an LFT belief is inconsistent with reality. It is also illogical since it is a nonsensical conclusion from the person's implicit rational belief (for example, 'Because it would be very bad if I failed my driving test, I couldn't stand it if I did fail'). Finally, like musts and awfulizing beliefs, it is unconstructive since it will interfere with the person's taking effective action if the negative event that the person is facing can be changed and it will stop the person making a healthy adjustment if the situation cannot be changed.

Self-/other-acceptance vs self-/other-downing Acceptance beliefs are rational in the sense that they are again primarily flexible. In discussing acceptance beliefs, we will focus on self-acceptance, although exactly the same arguments apply to other-acceptance. When a person accepts herself, she acknowledges that she is a unique, ongoing, ever-changing fallible human being with good, bad and neutral aspects. In short, she is far too complex to merit a single, global rating. Self-esteem, on the other hand, is based on the idea that it is possible to assign a single rating to the 'self'. An example of a self-acceptance belief expressed in its full form follows: 'If I fail my driving test due to my own errors, I could still accept myself as a fallible human being who has failed on this occasion. I would not be a failure.' As this example shows, a self-acceptance belief is consistent with the reality of a person being too complex to merit a single global rating. A self-acceptance belief is also logical since it is logical for a person to conclude that she is fallible if she makes errors. Finally, as with the other three rational beliefs I have discussed, a self-acceptance belief is constructive since it will once again help the person take effective action if the negative event that the person is facing can be changed and it will also aid the person to make a healthy adjustment if the situation cannot be changed.

Self-downing beliefs, on the other hand, are irrational in the sense that they take a rigid, grossly exaggerated view of the 'self'. They are couched in such statements as 'I am bad', 'I am a failure', 'I am less worthy', 'I am undeserving'. When a person holds a self-downing belief, she is working on the assumption that it is legitimate to assign a global (in this case, negative) rating to her 'self'. Since this in fact cannot be legitimately done, a self-downing belief is inconsistent with reality. It is also illogical since in making a self-downing statement, the person is making the 'part–whole error'; that is, she is correctly rating an aspect of herself, but then she rates her entire self based on the evaluation of the part. Finally, like the other three irrational beliefs we have discussed, a self-downing belief is unconstructive since it will interfere with the person taking effective action if the negative event that the person is facing can be changed and it will stop the person making a healthy adjustment if the situation cannot be changed.

Having now introduced the four rational beliefs and four irrational beliefs deemed by REBC theory to lie at the core of psychological well-being and psychological disturbance respectively, let us formally state the specific principle of emotional responsibility:

> The REBC specific principle of emotional responsibility states that events contribute to the way we feel and act, but do not cause these reactions which are largely determined by our rational or irrational beliefs about these events.

The two types of psychological disturbance

Having outlined the four irrational beliefs that underpin psychological disturbance, we will now proceed to discuss the two different types of such disturbance: ego disturbance and discomfort disturbance.

Ego disturbance

As the name implies, ego disturbance concerns psychological problems that ultimately relate to the person's view of herself. Sometimes such problems are obviously related to the self, as when a person is depressed and says, almost without prompting: 'Because I failed my driving test, I am a failure.' At other times, ego disturbance is not so transparent. For example, a person might claim to be anxious about travelling by underground. Put like that, it is not at all obvious that the person's problem may be an example of ego disturbance. However, on much closer examination, this turns out to be the case when the person reveals that he is anxious about travelling by tube because he might get panicky and, as stated in his own words, 'I might make a fool of myself by passing out.' Effective REBC is based on an accurate assessment of a client's problems and this assessment will reveal whether or not a particular problem is related to ego disturbance.

As discussed above, ego disturbance occurs when a person makes a global, negative rating of one's self. Such ratings can be made in different areas and are related to different disorders. Let us provide a few examples to illustrate our point.

1 When a person believes that he is a failure or a loser then it is likely that he will be depressed when he has failed or anxious when there exists a threat of failure which has not yet occurred.
2 When a person believes that he is bad then it is likely that he will experience guilt.
3 When a person believes that he is defective or weak then it is likely that he will experience shame.

The self-ratings that are involved in ego disturbance are usually expressed quite starkly, as in the statements: 'I am bad' or 'I am a bad person'. However, they can also be expressed more subtly as in the statements: 'I am less worthy' or 'I am undeserving'. Generally speaking, the more starkly they are expressed in the person's belief structure, the greater that person's ego disturbance will be.

Finally, as noted above, ego disturbance is derived from dogmatic musturbatory beliefs as in the following example: 'I am a failure because I did not pass my driving test as I absolutely should have done.' According to this view, if the person in this example had a preferential belief about failing, such as: 'I would have preferred not to have failed my driving test, but there's no reason why I absolutely should not have done', then he would be far less likely to condemn himself than he would if he held a demanding belief about failure as shown at the beginning of this paragraph.

Discomfort disturbance

As the name implies, discomfort disturbance concerns psychological problems that ultimately relate to the person's sense of comfort and discomfort. In REBC, the concepts of comfort and discomfort cover a wide range of issues. For example, they may relate to justice/injustice, fulfilment/frustration, positive feelings/negative feelings, etc. What they have in common, however, is that they do not refer to the person's view of himself. Rather, as the name implies, discomfort disturbance relates to the person's perceived inability to tolerate discomfort, whether this is in the area of feelings (such as anxiety) or life situations (such as unfairness).

Like ego disturbance, discomfort disturbance can be obvious or more subtle. An example of discomfort disturbance that is obvious is when a person says that he cannot stand waiting for the traffic lights to change. A more subtle example of discomfort disturbance is when a person says that he is afraid of failing his driving test. It might appear, at first sight, that the person's anxiety is an example of ego disturbance. However, on much closer examination, this turns out not to be the case when the person reveals that he is anxious about not getting the thousand pounds that his father promised him if he passed the test: 'I couldn't bear to lose out on all the goodies I had planned to buy with the money.' This is clearly an example of discomfort disturbance. As we mentioned earlier, careful assessment is needed to tease out discomfort disturbance-related irrational beliefs.

Discomfort disturbance occurs when a person has LFT beliefs. Such beliefs can be held in different areas and related to different disorders. Let us provide a few examples to illustrate this point.

1   When a person believes that he cannot stand being blocked or frustrated then it is likely that he will be angry.
2   When a person believes that he cannot tolerate losing a prized possession then it is likely that he will experience depression if he loses it.
3   When a person believes that he cannot bear feeling anxious then it is likely that he will experience increased anxiety.

The evaluations that are involved in discomfort disturbance can be explicit, as when the person says that he cannot bear the discomfort of speaking in public. However, they can also be implicit, as when people avoid facing uncomfortable situations. It is as if the person is implicitly saying 'I'll avoid that situation because I couldn't stand the discomfort of facing it'. The more widespread the person's avoidance, the greater that person's discomfort disturbance is likely to be.

Finally, as noted above, discomfort disturbance is derived from dogmatic musturbatory beliefs, as in the following example: 'I can't stand being deprived because I absolutely must get what I want.' As discussed in the section on ego disturbance, if the person in this example had a preferential belief about being deprived, such as 'I would like to get what I want, but I don't have to get it', then he would be far less likely to disturb himself about the deprivation than he would if he held a demanding belief about his failure to get what he wants.

Ego disturbance and discomfort disturbance can interact

Ego disturbance and discomfort disturbance can interact, often in complex ways. For example, let us suppose that a person believes that he must do well at a job interview and if he does not that means that he is less worthy than he would be if he did well. This ego disturbance belief leads the person to feel anxiety as the date of the interview draws near. At this point the person becomes aware that he is feeling anxious and tells himself implicitly that he must get rid of his anxiety straight away and that he cannot stand feeling anxious. As the result of this discomfort disturbance belief, his anxiety increases. Realizing that he is getting very anxious for what to him is no good reason and that he absolutely should not do this, he concludes that he is a weak, pathetic person for getting matters out of proportion. This ego disturbance adds to his emotional distress which activates fears, discomfort-related irrational beliefs, about losing control.

It is important to note that this interaction between ego disturbance and discomfort disturbance can occur very quickly and outside the person's awareness. Dealing therapeutically with complex interactions between the two types of disturbance as exemplified above is quite difficult and involves the therapist dealing with one link of the chain at a time.

The ABCDE of REBC

You will find the ABCDEs of REBC in virtually every book that has been published on rational emotive behavioural counselling and here we will briefly describe what this means.

A

A stands for an **activating event** which triggers your client's rational or irrational beliefs, which in turn determine her feelings and the way she acts. A's can be actual events or inferences (that is, hypotheses about actual events which may be correct or incorrect, but which need testing out). Furthermore, A's can be external events or internal events (for example, bodily sensations) and can stand for past, present or future events.

B

B stands for your client's rational and irrational **beliefs** which are evaluative in nature. We have already presented the four major types of rational and irrational beliefs as they are featured in REBC (see pp. viii–xii). While some REBC therapists prefer to place all cognitive activity under B, it is our practice to put only rational and irrational beliefs under B and to put other cognitions (for example, inferences) at A.

C

C stands for **consequences** and represents the person's emotional and/or behavioural response to the beliefs she holds about the event (or inference) in question. In REBC theory, negative emotions can be healthy (as when they are based on rational beliefs about A) or unhealthy (as when they are based on irrational beliefs about A). For further information about healthy and unhealthy negative emotions see Dryden (1990).

It is easy to forget that C also represents a behavioural response. Sometimes your client will exhibit self-defeating behaviour based on a set of irrational beliefs she holds about A. When this occurs either the behaviour occurs without corresponding emotion or it is designed to 'ward off' your client's disturbed feelings.

D

D stands for **disputing**. In particular it stands for disputing your client's irrational beliefs by asking questions that encourage the person to question the empirical, logical and pragmatic status of her irrational beliefs. We will discuss disputing strategies in point 12.

E

E stands for the **effects** of disputing. When disputing is successful it helps the client to change her feelings and actions at C and change her thinking at B. In addition, when disputing is successful, it helps the person to make more functional inferences at A.

Having spelled out the ABCDEs of REBC, we will now show how some of these interact in complex ways.

The principle of psychological interactionism

So far you can be forgiven if you think that REBC considers that thinking, feeling and behaviour are separate psychological systems. However, this is far from the case. When Albert Ellis originated REBC in the mid-1950s (when it was first known as rational psychotherapy), he put forward the view that thinking (including imagery), feeling and behaviour are interdependent, interacting psychological processes.

Thus, when a person experiences an emotion at C, he has the tendency to think and act in a certain way. Also when someone holds a rational or irrational belief (at B) about a negative event (at A), this will influence his feelings and behaviours (at C). Finally, if a person acts in a certain way, this will be related to his feelings and thoughts.

What follows on from this is, first, that REBC counsellors need to pay close attention to thoughts, feelings and behaviour in the assessment process, and secondly, that they need to use a variety of cognitive, emotive and behavioural techniques in the intervention phase of counselling.

The process of therapeutic change

In order to practise REBC effectively, it is important to have an understanding of the process of therapeutic change. This knowledge will help you to use REBC interventions in the most appropriate sequence. We will briefly mention the steps that clients need to take in REBC to experience therapeutic change, before discussing each step in greater detail. While we will put these steps in a certain order, please note that this order is not a rigid one and should certainly not be applied rigidly in counselling. Also, there will be problems along the way since therapeutic change is rarely, if ever, a smooth process (see point 19).

1 Understanding the specific principle of emotional responsibility.
2 Understanding the determinants of one's psychological problems.
3 Setting goals and committing oneself to achieving them.
4 Understanding and committing oneself to the REBC means of achieving one's goals.
5 Putting this learning into practice.
6 Maintaining these gains.

Understanding the specific principle of emotional responsibility

We discussed this principle at length at the beginning of this chapter, so we will not repeat ourselves. However, it is important to stress that if your clients do not grasp or do not accept this principle, then they will derive little benefit from REBC.

Understanding the determinants of one's psychological problems

This step involves you and your client pooling resources to apply the specific principle of emotional responsibility to illuminate the determinants of the client's emotional problems. This involves you helping your client to specify her problems and give examples of these problems so that these can be assessed. Assessment is directed towards identifying unhealthy emotions, the actual or inferred events that provide the context for these emotions, the behaviours that the client enacts when she is experiencing her unhealthy emotions and, most importantly, the irrational beliefs that lie at the core of the client's problems. Unless your client understands the determinants of her problems and agrees with this assessment, REBC will falter at this point.

Setting goals and committing oneself to achieving them

An important part of therapeutic change is setting goals and committing time, energy and effort to taking the necessary steps to achieving them. Let us consider each of these points in turn.

Goal-setting There is an old adage that says: 'If you don't know where you're going, you won't know when you've got there.'

This points to the importance of setting goals in the therapeutic change process. Bordin (1979) noted that agreement on therapeutic goals is an important therapeutic ingredient and one part of a tripartite view of the working alliance that has gained much prominence in psychotherapy research (Horvath and Greenberg, 1994). In REBC you should help your client to set goals which are: specific, realistic, achievable, measurable and which aid her overall psychological well-being. Your client should 'own' her goals, which means that she should set them primarily for her own well-being and not to please anybody else (for example, significant others or you as counsellor).

However, as an REBC counsellor, you have an important goal for your client and it is very important that you are open about this and discuss it frankly with her. This goal involves your client learning and practising the skills of what might be called REBC self-help counselling so that she can use them after counselling has ended. Indeed, your role as an REBC counsellor is to give away to your clients as much of REBC as they are able to learn. You will, of course, have to help your clients understand that learning these skills will help them to achieve their therapeutic goals, otherwise they will have little interest in learning them. As Bordin (1979) noted, helping your clients to see the relevance of your and their therapeutic tasks to achieving their goals is a central part of the process of REBC. Not all clients will want to learn these self-help skills and you can help them (albeit less effectively) without teaching them these skills. However, if you do not offer this opportunity to your clients, they will certainly not be able to take advantage of it!

Making a commitment to achieve goals   Goal-setting will be an academic exercise unless your clients are prepared to commit themselves to achieving their goals. A major reason why people do not keep to their new year resolutions for very long is that they are not prepared to do what is necessary to achieve what they have resolved to achieve. They want the gain without the pain. So as part of the goal-setting process, discuss with your clients how much time, effort and energy they will have to expend in order to achieve their goals. Then ask them if they are willing to make such an investment. If they are, then you may wish to make a formal agreement with them to this effect. If they are not prepared to make the necessary investment, then you will have to set new goals in line with the kind of investment they are prepared to make. Of course, this may all change once your work with your client has advanced. Nevertheless, it is important to get

REBC off on the right foot in this respect. So, in short, set goals with your clients that they are prepared to commit to before you do any further counselling with them.

Understanding and committing oneself to the REBC means of achieving one's goals

After you have agreed with your client goals to which she is prepared to commit herself, you then have to ensure that she understands your suggestions concerning how these goals can best be reached. This is the aspect of REBC where the technical nature of counselling comes to the fore. REBC does have definite suggestions concerning what clients need to do in order to achieve their goals. These suggestions take the form of specific techniques. In order for clients to understand the nature of REBC in this respect, you need to be able to explain what you are going to do in counselling and what is expected of your client in ways that are clear and detailed. You want clients to proceed with counselling having made an informed decision about REBC. In your description you need to stress two things. First, you need to show your client how putting into practice the technical aspects of the counselling will help her to achieve her goals. Secondly, you need to explain what investments with respect to time, energy and effort your client needs to make in putting REBC techniques into practice.

We have found it very useful at this juncture to point out to clients that there exist other approaches to counselling and that if what we have to offer does not make sense to the person, if she does not think that REBC will be helpful to her or if she thinks it involves too much of an investment for her, then we suggest other therapeutic possibilities, discuss these with the client and make a judicious referral.

Putting this learning into practice

It is not sufficient for clients to understand that they have to put REBC techniques into practice, nor even to commit themselves to so doing. They actually have to do it. Otherwise they will have 'intellectual insight', which in this context may be seen as a light and occasionally held conviction that their irrational beliefs are irrational and their rational beliefs are rational. While this 'intellectual insight' is important to have, it is insufficient to help clients to achieve their goals. For this to occur, clients need a fair measure of what might be called 'emotional insight', which in this context is the same realization about rational and irrational beliefs as in 'intellectual insight', but one which is strongly and frequently held. It is this 'emotional insight' which affects a person's feelings and influences his behaviour and this is the true goal of clients putting their learning into practice in their everyday lives.

There are several dimensions of between-session practice that are important here:

1 Repetition. It is important for clients to go over new rational beliefs many times before they begin to believe them. This repetition applies to the use of cognitive, emotive and behavioural techniques.
2 Force and energy. One useful way that clients can move from intellectual insight to emotional insight is to employ techniques with force and energy. However, it is important that they can understand and see the relevance of particular rational beliefs before forcefully and energetically working to internalize them.
3 Vividness. The use of what I (W.D.) have called vivid techniques in REBC (Dryden, 1986) can help clients to remember their rational beliefs more than standard, non-vivid techniques. Vividness tends to increase the impact of rational concepts and thus makes it easier for clients to retrieve them from memory at times when it is necessary to do so. As such, they will get more practice at thinking rationally than they would ordinarily do.

Ordinarily, it is important for REBC counsellors to take great care when they negotiate homework assignments with their clients (see point 22). However, no matter how careful you are when negotiating such assignments, your clients may still have difficulty putting them into practice. As such, an important part of encouraging clients to put their therapy-derived insights into practice is helping them to identify and overcome such obstacles (see point 27).

Maintaining therapeutic gains

Once your clients have achieved their goals, this is not the end of the therapeutic story, although many of your clients will think or hope that it is. If they have such thoughts and hopes then they will stop using the principles that you have taught them and thus increase the chances that they will experience a lapse or, more seriously, a relapse. We define a lapse as a minor return to the problem state, while a relapse is a major return to this state. If your clients are to maintain their therapeutic gains they have to be helped to do so and take responsibility for this maintenance work themselves. This involves first relapse prevention and secondly spreading the effect of change.

Relapse prevention   It is important to deal with relapse prevention before the end of REBC, otherwise the client may not be prepared for the re-emergence of his problems. As mentioned above, it is rare for clients not to experience lapses, and if they do, they need prior help to deal with a lapse when it occurs. If a lapse, or a series of lapses, is not dealt with it may lead to a relapse since relapses tend to occur when lapses are not identified and dealt with by the person concerned. Relapse prevention, therefore, involves the following steps.

1   Recognizing that lapses are likely to occur and thinking rationally about this point.
2   Identifying the likely contexts in which lapses are likely to occur and problem-solving each salient element.
3   Exposing oneself to the problematic contexts and using the problem-solving skills previously learned to prevent the development of the lapse.
4   Committing oneself to continue this process for as long as necessary.

If the worst comes to the worst and a relapse does occur, then you should help your client to think rationally about this grim reality and understanding of how this developed should be sought, before further treatment decisions are made.

If it looks unlikely that your client will achieve her therapeutic goals by the end of counselling, it is still worthwhile raising the issue of relapse prevention, although necessarily this will have to be done rather theoretically, with perhaps a written handout on relapse prevention supplementing your verbal explanation. You will need to do this after you have helped your client to formulate a plan which she can follow to achieve her goals after therapy has formally ended.

Spreading the effect of change   Another important way of helping to ensure that your client maintains her gains is to encourage her to practise what she has learned about overcoming her problems in certain contexts in other contexts. Thus, if a client has overcome her fear of refusing unreasonable requests at work and is

1   Be flexible in your use of the bond aspects of REBC

This first section of the present text is devoted to developing and maintaining a therapeutic alliance. Bordin (1979) has argued that there are three important components of the alliance: **goals** (which represent what your client wishes to gain from counselling); **tasks** (which are the activities that you and your client engage in to help your client achieve her goals); and **bonds** (which reflect the quality of the interpersonal relationship between you and your client). Herein we focus on the bond aspects of REBC. Discussion of goals and tasks as they relate to REBC can be found in points 2 and 3.

In our view writers on REBC have tended to overemphasize the technical aspects of this approach to counselling and to underemphasize its relationship aspects. While REBC therapists might like to think that the bond aspects of this approach to counselling are relatively unimportant, our view is that they are a core ingredient of the therapeutic impact that REBC counsellors have on their clients. Indeed, a recent research study showed that REBC counsellors were rated at least as high on the facilitative core conditions of empathy, respect and genuineness as counsellors who were more relationship-oriented in approach (DiGiuseppe et al., 1993). To what extent this finding correlates with positive outcomes remains to be seen. However, it does show that clients are aware of the human qualities of their REBC counsellors even though the therapeutic power of these qualities is not emphasized in the REBC literature.

What is the preferred counsellor–client relationship in REBC?

Every therapeutic orientation suggests a preferred relationship between counsellor and client even though it recognizes that it may not always be possible to establish this preferred relationship. But what is the preferred therapeutic relationship in REBC? Albert Ellis, the founder of REBC, is quite clear on this point. He argues that the preferred counsellor–client relationship has the following features.

- REBC has a large pedagogical element where the counsellor *teaches* the client the ABCs of REBC and helps her to see how she disturbs herself and what she can do to undisturb herself.
- REBC is based on an *informal, businesslike* bond where two adults get down to the business of helping one of them to live more healthily. In this relationship the counsellor and client are equal in their humanity, but unequal in their knowledge and expertise on psychological disturbance and well-being.
- The REBC counsellor shows the client *unconditional acceptance* and teaches her to apply this concept to herself in her everyday life.
- The REBC counsellor is not unduly warm to his client, since this may reinforce the latter's dire need for approval and may distract her from initiating and maintaining the difficult journey towards greater psychological well-being.

Varying the therapeutic bond in REBC

Having outlined the preferred counsellor–client relationship in REBC, it should be noted that different clients do require different bonds in this type of therapy. Let us discuss two examples of such bond variations.

Formal–informal

While REBC counsellors prefer to have an informal (although problem-solving orientated) relationship with their clients, they can offer a more formal bond with those clients who would appear to benefit from it. Offering a more formal bond can involve such things as addressing your client by her surname, using your surname with her, wearing formal, professional clothing in counselling sessions, using formal language and refraining from the use of profane language.

Some clients may, of course, do better in REBC if you are more informal in your mode of interaction than you would ordinarily be. This may again involve making suitable changes in your dress, but may also involve modifications in your seating arrangements (for example, sitting on cushions instead of on chairs or putting your feet up on a desk) and in your non-verbal behaviour. In addition, with such clients you might use self-disclosure and humour more than with other clients. Let us stress one point here, however: whatever changes you make in your behaviour, do not contravene your code of professional ethics. For instance, do not form a friendship or love relationship with your clients.

Expert impact – personal impact

Linked to the issue of developing formal and informal bonds with clients is the issue of the source of your impact with clients. It would be nice if your clients would just respond to the rational concepts that you will be teaching them, but humans are not just affected by the message; they will listen to a message more attentively if they respect the source of that message. Consequently, you will need to ask yourself whether your clients are more likely to listen to you if they respect your expertise or if they like you as a person.

Thus, some clients will respond to your expertise and will be impressed by your qualifications, any books or articles that you have written and by a variety of other professional accoutrements which serve to label you as an expert in the client's mind. Such clients are basically saying, 'I'll listen to this person. She obviously knows what she is talking about'. Other clients, on the other hand, will not be at all impressed by your expertise, but will be more concerned with your personal qualities and whether or not they like you as a person. These clients are basically saying, 'I like this person so I'll listen to him'. You may have a great many qualifications and a string of letters after your name, or have written as many books as Albert Ellis, but if a client does not like you, he will not listen to you.

Emphasizing your expertise is a matter of displaying your diplomas and professional awards, suggesting to clients that they read books or articles that you have written and generally creating the atmosphere of an expert professional. On the other hand, relying on your likeability involves discovering which personal characteristics your clients will best respond to and then emphasizing these in your interactions with these clients.

All this may sound very Machiavellian, but we maintain that human beings do this all the time in their relationships with other people, that is to say we emphasize different aspects of ourselves with different people at different times. Given this, there is no good reason why we should show a restricted interactive range in counselling. As long as we are genuine, we can become what Arnold Lazarus (1981) calls an 'authentic chameleon' in our work with our clients. Finally, if you do not think you can provide a client with a particular therapeutic bond that she requires, then it is important to effect a suitable referral to another counsellor.

Discovering the right bond

We wish that we could give you an easy recipe for discovering which bond will be most effective with which client, but we cannot. However, we can suggest certain guidelines to help you in this respect.

Ask the client

George Kelly, the originator of personal construct therapy, has often been quoted as saying, 'If you want to know anything about your client, ask him. He just might tell you.' Thus, you might ask your client such direct questions as:

- 'What kind of therapeutic relationship do you think would be most helpful to you?'
- 'Do you think it is more important that your therapist has expertise or is a likeable person?'
- 'Do you think you would respond better to a therapist who is formal or informal in his/her interactive style?'
- 'Have you had counselling or therapy before? If so and if it was a helpful experience for you, what were the qualities of the counsellor or therapist that were helpful?'

In addition, you might ask a number of indirect questions, the answers to which may suggest the kind of therapeutic bond that is best for a particular client.

- 'In your life, who has been instrumental in helping you to develop as a person? What did they do that was helpful? What qualities did they have that you found therapeutic?'
- 'Have you had the experience of being positively helped when you were feeling emotionally distressed about something? If so, what were the qualities of the other person that you found helpful?'
- 'Who are the people in your life who have been naturally therapeutic to you? What were their qualities?'

You can ask your client these questions directly or put these items on any questionnaire that you ask your client to complete.

Knowledge of your client's psychopathology

Another way of calibrating the bond that you seek to develop with your client is to understand the interpersonal features of certain psychological disorders. A few examples will illustrate what we mean. If your client has a histrionic personality, it is important that you refrain from developing a bond that might exacerbate his excitable personality. Thus, you should be calm and use techniques which defuse his tendency to get overexcited. On the other hand, if your client is obsessive–compulsive in personality organization, you should strive to introduce affect into your sessions, but do so gradually, otherwise you will frighten the client away. Thus, you should gradually increase your level of warmth and the flamboyant aspects of your own personality. Finally, if your client has a borderline personality organization, which is marked by sudden shifts of strong affect, you should model a consistent and empathic approach rooted in your use of firm boundaries.

Two points are important here. First, you should acquaint yourself with the interpersonal dimensions of different person-ality structures, and secondly, you should respect the subtle individual differences that occur within each structure. If, in working with specific clients, you are unsure concerning the type of bond to establish, we highly recommend that you take such cases to supervision (see point 29).

Feedback on bond behaviour

It is important that you consider the decisions you make about bond variation as tentative and open to modification. One way to do this is to elicit feedback on your bond behaviour from your clients. Thus, at the end of a session, you might ask your client such questions as:

• 'How would you describe the way I am interacting with you? Has this been helpful or unhelpful?'
• 'How would you like me to interact with you? How would this be more helpful to you?'

If you are concerned about the impact of any aspect of your bond behaviour, ask directly about this. For example:

- 'If you recall, I told you a little about my way of dealing with a problem similar to yours. How did you react to this?'
- 'I've been trying to inject some humour into our sessions; how have you responded to this?'
- 'You may have noticed that I have adopted a fairly business-like attitude in our sessions. Has this been helpful to you or not?'

You will, of course, explore your clients' answers to such questions so that you can understand better the reasons for their responses and you will need to think carefully about the implications of their answers. We are not advocating that you adopt a naive approach and that you should accept uncritically your clients' points and change your behaviour accordingly. Rather, we suggest that you listen with respect to what your clients say and change your behaviour when you consider that it is therapeutic to do so.

Key point

Be aware that you will need to vary the bond that you develop with your clients. In doing so, take into account their preferences and their predominant personality features, and elicit feedback from them concerning their reactions to salient dimensions of the therapeutic relationship.

---

2   Ensure that your clients have reasonable, self-helping goals for their REBC

A great many clients are quite naive as to just how counselling may be of help to them. Some may have little or no notion as to what to expect, while others may show up for their first appointment with preconceived (and quite inaccurate) ideas about what they can hope to gain from the counselling process. Influenced by media portrayals of counselling and psychotherapy, they may expect that their counselling experience will somehow magically provide them with the keys to serenity and happiness.

When clients enter into REBC, it is important for you to check to see that they have reasonable, self-helping goals for their counselling. If you are trying to help a client work toward what you regard as quite reasonable goals for counselling, but your client is interested in pursuing an entirely different set of goals, it is likely that you will waste valuable counselling time and eventually encounter 'resistance'. As an example, your client may neglect to do a particular homework assignment that you have suggested because she is unable to see how it will help her to achieve her goals. Early on in counselling, it is important to check that you and your client are in agreement on the goals you will be working toward. In the following sections we review some of the common types of potentially self-defeating goals with which clients may enter REBC, as well as techniques for helping to ensure that client goals are self-helping and not self-defeating.

Commonly encountered self-defeating client goals

Some of the potentially self-defeating goals with which naive clients frequently enter REBC can be categorized as follows.

1   The goal of changing negative activating events (A's) (as opposed to working to modify dysfunctional beliefs and feelings).
2   The goal of doing away with all negative feelings (with a failure to recognize that some types of negative feelings may actually be self-helping).
3   The goal of simply attaining 'insight' into why one functions as one does.
4   The goal of simply attending counselling sessions in order that the counsellor might somehow 'fix' the client's presenting problems.

Each of these categories will be treated separately.

The goal of changing negative A's

A significant number of new clients will view counselling mainly as a vehicle for modifying the negative activating events in their lives. Thus, a given client may enter REBC and express the following goal to her counsellor: 'I want to improve my interpersonal skills so that I'm less likely to experience rejections in social situations.' Rather than working on overcoming her anxiety about the possibility of experiencing a rejection experience, this client wants to focus on decreasing the probability that a negative activating event of this sort will occur. From the REBC perspective, it would be preferable for the client to work on her anxiety as well as work to improve her social skills. This is because (a) it is unlikely that even with improved social skills she will *never* experience another rejection, and (b) she will be less likely to deploy her new skills in social situations if she continues to make herself anxious about the prospect of being rejected. REBC counsellors can explain to clients like this that it is advisable to work at making themselves less disturbable (by modifying their disturbance-producing beliefs) with respect to their negative activating events, as it is improbable that they will be able to exert complete control over the occurrence of such events in their lives.

The goal of eliminating all negative feelings

Other clients may enter counselling with the goal of completely eradicating all types of negatively toned feelings. As an example, a male client with anger problems may indicate that he wants to feel completely calm when he responds to the misbehaviour of his 7-year-old son. This, however, would not represent a reasonable goal in REBC terms, as it is unlikely that he will (a) face episodes of misbehaviour with complete calm as long as he strongly desires that his son behave appropriately, and (b) be very motivated to respond to episodes of misbehaviour with effective and consistent discipline if he does not feel at least mildly annoyed when they occur. In order to achieve a state of 'complete calmness', this father would have to give up his preference for appropriate behaviour on his son's part and replace it with an 'I really don't care' attitude. REBC typically does not focus on changing clients' basic wants, preferences and desires, and holds that many sorts of negative feelings (such as annoyance, concern and regret) are actually quite healthy and functional since they motivate us to change those elements of unpleasant circumstances that can be changed (Dryden and Yankura, 1993). When working with clients who express the goal of doing away with all negative feelings, it is a good idea to explain the distinction that REBC makes between healthy and unhealthy negative emotions, and to make sure that clients understand why healthy negative emotions can be constructive and self-enhancing.

The goal of attaining 'curative' insight

Other individuals may begin their counselling with the notion that if they can just attain 'deep insights' as to why they feel and act dysfunctionally, their emotional and behavioural problems will spontaneously melt away. Such clients may have had prior exposure (either through actual experience or through the media) to 'insight-oriented' therapies such as psychoanalysis. It is advisable for counsellors to explain carefully that insight alone (whether of the REBC variety or some other sort) rarely results in meaningful and lasting change, and that greater benefits are likely to accrue from counselling when clients concertedly work at challenging and replacing their upset-producing irrational beliefs. If a given client proves unwilling to accept this explanation and to work in this fashion (at least on a trial basis), it may be appropriate to refer him or her to a practitioner who offers the type of approach they are seeking.

The goal of being 'fixed' by the counsellor

Finally, some clients will start counselling with the idea that you will somehow magically 'fix' them – their goal is simply to present their bodies at your office at the time specified for their appointment. This, of course, is not in line with the REBC approach, which holds that clients will tend to make gains in counselling in proportion to the efforts that they make at changing. It is important for counsellors to make clear to clients that REBC is a *collaborative* venture, and that while the counsellor will help the client to identify what needs to be worked on and will assist in designing ways to work on it, it is essentially up to the client to be an active participant during counselling sessions and to implement homework assignments during the interval between sessions. Counsellors can often help clients to identity and deal with psychological obstacles to being active participants within their own counselling (see, for example, points 18 and 19), but meaningful change is rarely accomplished easily and clients will often have to 'push' themselves to face the discomfort involved in changing. It is clearly desirable for clients to understand this early on in the REBC counselling process.

Techniques for ensuring that clients have self-helping goals

Two helpful ways for making sure that clients have reasonable goals for their REBC are (a) to encourage clients to construct a problem list, and (b) to jointly set session agendas.

Constructing a problem list

In one of the early sessions of counselling, clients can be asked to undertake the homework assignment of writing down the various problems they would like to give attention to in their counselling. You can then work collaboratively with your clients during counselling sessions to translate the problems contained on their lists into counselling goals. This time spent working on translating problems into goals provides you with a good opportunity to assess whether a given client has reasonable goals in mind for counselling, and allows you to suggest goals that are likely to be self-helping for your client.

Setting session agendas

You can also promote the routine of collaboratively setting session agendas at the start of each counselling session. Here, you would ask your client the following sort of question: 'What problem would you like to devote most of today's session to working on?' If your client responds by presenting a reasonable goal, this can become the focus of the session; if not, you can work with your client to develop a goal that is more appropriate for REBC.

Key point

Clients new to REBC may present unreasonable, potentially self-defeating goals for their counselling. Thus, it is important for counsellors to assess clients' goals and to help them formulate more appropriate ones if necessary. Encouraging clients to set session agendas and to construct problem lists can be useful ways of checking on their goals.

---

3 Ensure that you and your clients understand each other's tasks and can execute them effectively

In REBC, both you and your clients have a number of tasks to perform. In the brief overview that we presented on REBC in the Introduction, we listed what these tasks are. Our purpose here is to underscore the point that it is important that you and your clients develop a mutual understanding of your respective tasks and make a commitment to performing them. Since REBC has a decided educational emphasis, it is perhaps easier for you to do this than it would be for counsellors who practise an approach to counselling that is not so explicitly educational in nature. As such, you can educate your clients directly on this point and discuss openly their reactions. Let us now outline the issues that you need to consider when addressing task behaviour in REBC.

Explain what your principal tasks are as an REBC counsellor

REBC is an approach to counselling that is based on the value of being explicit with clients. While counsellors from other orientations may be happy to perform their tasks and hope that their clients may correctly infer why they act as they do, as an REBC counsellor you will not be content with this. This is because you will appreciate that your clients may form incorrect inferences about your task behaviour which may have a deleterious effect on the counselling process. Instead, whenever feasible and without doing so compulsively, we suggest that you explain to your clients what you will be doing and provide a plausible rationale concerning why you are doing it.

For example, before you dispute a client's irrational beliefs you might say something like this.

> Now that we have identified the key beliefs that underpin your guilt feelings, I'd like to ask you a number of questions which are designed

to help you reevaluate these beliefs. In doing so, I'll help you to stick to the point. The reason for my questioning behaviour is this. My questions will help you to think for yourself about the usefulness, logic and accuracy of these ideas and this will help you to begin to develop beliefs that are more useful for you, more logical and are more consistent with reality. Does that make sense to you?

You will note that this example shows three things. The counsellor (i) told the client what she was going to do, (ii) explained why she was going to do it and (iii) asked for the client's reaction. This last point is important. Unless your client understands for himself what your task is your explanation will not have had its desired effect. Let us stress one point here: while we have presented the counsellor's explanation in a didactic form, you may well prefer to explain your task more Socratically and 'tease out' the responses you are looking for from your client while encouraging him to think about the issues you raise. Whether you educate Socratically or didactically, you will need to do so whenever you execute a principal REBC task.

Help your clients to understand what their principal tasks are in REBC

Every approach to counselling calls upon clients to perform tasks that are deemed therapeutic by that approach. REBC is no exception and we outlined in the Introduction the principal tasks that your clients have to execute if they are to benefit from this approach. Let us demonstrate how you might do this.

Now that I have helped you to dispute your belief that your neighbour absolutely must consider your feelings and you can now see that a healthier belief would be: 'I would very much like my neighbour to consider my feelings, but he doesn't have to', let me suggest how you might take this forward. The next time that you find yourself making yourself angry about your neighbour's lack of consideration for your feelings, really look for the demand you are making about his behaviour. Write this demand down and ask yourself the three questions that I asked you: 'Is my demand consistent with reality?'; 'Does it follow logically from my preference?' and 'Is my demand helping me to solve my conflict with him?' Really think through your answers and then remind yourself of your healthier rational belief. The reason I am suggesting that you do this for yourself is that doing so will help you to become increasingly proficient at identifying, challenging and changing those ideas that underpin what you call your temper. What do you think of my suggestion?

Again note that the counsellor (i) has explained what she wanted the client to do, (ii) given him a rationale for the task and (iii) asked for feedback. Once again please note that while we have presented this as a monologue, in clinical practice you would involve your client in an ongoing interchange on this issue. Finally, we suggest that you use these three guidelines whenever addressing your clients' principal tasks in REBC.

Other issues

A comprehensive discussion of the issues concerning counsellor and client tasks would require far more space than we have here. So we will conclude this point by mentioning some of these issues in brief.

1   Help your client to see how executing his tasks will help him to achieve his therapeutic goals.

Your client may understand what his tasks are, but may not see how executing them is related to his goals for change (see point 2). Help him to do so, otherwise he will not execute them or will do so only half-heartedly.

2   Only ask your client to perform tasks that he is actually capable of achieving.

If you ask your client to do something which he is incapable of doing, you will contribute to his demoralization, which may lead to his dropping out of counselling or deteriorating while remaining in therapy. Thus, ensure that you assess your client's abilities accurately and only suggest tasks that he is able to do.

3   Help your client to see that he is capable of executing those tasks that he is able to do.

Your client may understand the nature of his principal tasks, see clearly that doing them will help him to achieve his therapeutic goals and be actually able to carry them out, but he still may not do them because he *believes* that he is not capable of executing them. Help him to develop this belief, for example, by breaking the task down into smaller chunks and creating an opportunity for him to carry these out in the counselling session. In addition, you may have to encourage him to carry out the task unconfidently at first since doing so will help him to develop confidence later in his ability to carry out the task.

4   Help your client to see the close relationship between your tasks on the one hand and his tasks and goals on the other.

Maxie Maultsby (1984), an REBT psychiatrist, has said that good therapy encourages the client to practise effective self-therapy. This is the principle which underpins the relationship between your tasks, your client's tasks and his goals. The successful execution of your therapeutic tasks helps your client to carry out his tasks which in turn helps him to achieve his goals. Encouraging your client to see this three-cornered relationship helps him to understand that you are both working together in the service of his goals.

5   Ensure that you perform your tasks competently.

We believe that it is easy to practise REBC poorly. Therefore it is important that you ensure that you are performing your REBC tasks as competently as possible. You can do this by being properly trained in REBC and by being closely supervised by an REBC supervisor (see point 29). Doing so helps you not only to practise your tasks skilfully, it also increases your repertoire of potent REBC tasks. Having a broad repertoire helps you to vary your use of tasks according to client need and increases your therapeutic flexibility.

Key point

The function of therapeutic tasks is to help your clients achieve their goals. If you and your clients have a mutual understanding of each other's tasks and can execute them effectively, then the therapeutic potential of these tasks can be realized.

---

4   Work to operationalize vague client problems in REBC terms

Clients will often describe problems that brought them to counselling in rather vague and confusing ways. If you, as counsellor, neglect to take steps early on in the counselling process to operationalize vaguely expressed problems in REBC terms, you will encounter difficulty with accurately identifying suitable targets for change (that is, operative irrational beliefs and relevant dysfunctional emotions and behaviours). REBC's ABC model can help counsellors (and clients) to understand client problems in terms that facilitate the identification of self-helping counselling goals and relevant intervention strategies. Under this point we will review some frequently occurring categories of vaguely described client problems, and will then describe some guidelines (with an illustrative example) for using the ABC model to conceptualize vaguely expressed problems in a way that will facilitate the counselling process.

Examples of vaguely expressed client problems

Vague A or C

It is quite common for clients initially to refer to an emotional problem they are experiencing in overly general, vague terms. Thus, a given client may state during her first counselling session that 'I feel upset about the way my husband is handling our finances.' Here, it would be important to pinpoint the emotional C's that the client is actually experiencing, and to obtain more specific information about the A involved in the client's upset. This could be accomplished through your skilful use of questions. To identify a relevant A, you could ask the following sort of question: 'Can you give me a recent example of a time when you felt upset about the way your husband handles the finances?' In the present example, the client may respond by stating that she felt very upset when her husband went off on one of his frequent gambling sprees over the weekend. Having learned about a relevant (but still general) A to which your client is often exposed, you could then employ the following question (which, you will notice, is preceded by a didactic statement) in order to identify relevant C's: '"Upset" is really sort of a vague way to describe strong negative feeling that we may experience. Can you tell me more specifically what you were feeling when your husband left you at home to go off gambling?' This inquiry could lead to discussion which reveals that your client experiences anxiety about the possibility that her husband will gamble away all of their savings, and anger about the fact that he exposes the family to such financial risk.

Absent A or C

Clients will also often begin counselling with a description of their presenting complaints that omits either the A or the C of an ABC sequence relevant to their emotional problems. As an example of an absent A, a male client may enter counselling with the complaint, 'I find myself feeling anxious almost all of the time.' Again through skilful questioning, the counsellor might determine that this individual has a wide variety of A's that are implicated in his frequent anxiety episodes; for example, these A's could take the form of thoughts about the possibility of receiving social disapproval ('My boss might think I did a lousy job on the report I just submitted'; 'My friends may judge me harshly when they see what a mess my place is'; 'Jim probably thinks I'm a snob because I didn't say hello to him at the office this morning'). As an example of an absent C, another client may complain that, 'My job is too stressful: the boss is on my case nearly every day.' This client has presented a vague description of an A (about which the counsellor will want to obtain further details), but has omitted any description of the unhealthy negative feelings he experiences with respect to this A. Here, the counsellor will want to determine whether he experiences anxiety, shame, guilt, anger and/or depression with respect to his stressful job and critical boss. Some clients will lack the terminology or the sophistication to label the emotional C's they experience; in such cases, it can be important for the counsellor to provide them with an emotional vocabulary that is consonant with REBC theory (see point 5).

Problems that represent an ABC complex

Occasionally, when asked to describe the problem that brought them to counselling, clients will respond with a vague statement that actually represents an ABC complex. To cite an example, a given client may report: 'I feel trapped in my current job.' We do not, however, have an emotion called 'trapped', and it would be important to question the client in order clearly to define the A, B and C factors that actually comprise his problem.

Problems stated in popular terms

Clients may also latch on to currently popular phrases or terms in their initial attempts to describe their problems to you. When clients attribute their difficulties to such things as a 'mid-life crisis' or 'burn out', they may provide themselves with the illusion that they understand why they are suffering emotional distress. Such attributions may in some cases actually help to reduce their distress to some degree, as it is somewhat reassuring to have the knowledge that one is experiencing a 'popular' problem (that is, one that many other people have presumably experienced). However, problem descriptions phrased in popular terms do not lend themselves to effective rational emotive behavioural counselling, and it is again important for you to break down the client's problem into its A, B and C components.

Case example

Peter, a 36-year-old attorney for a large corporation, came to counselling complaining that he was suffering from 'burn out'. In order to begin conceptualizing his problem in ABC terms, his counsellor first employed a didactic statement followed by a question: 'Sometimes, when people say they're "burnt out", they mean that they're experiencing anxiety or depression. Have you been troubled more than usual by either of those two feelings?' In response to the counsellor's question, Peter acknowledged that he was frequently anxious with respect to his job. At this point, the counsellor has obtained some information about an emotional C and is in a good position to identify a relevant A. She thus asks her client, 'With respect to your job, what are you mainly feeling anxious about?' This inquiry prompts Peter to report that he has recently been promoted and now has to engage in many new tasks with which he lacks familiarity. He thinks that his superiors may come to regard him as incompetent, and that he will subsequently be demoted or fired. Peter further relates that he worries over these potential negative outcomes a good part of each day, both at work and at home. His counsellor decides for the time being to accept his thoughts about being demoted or fired as constituting a relevant A, and moves on to assessment of operative irrational beliefs. Through a combination of didactic and Socratic approaches, she establishes that Peter subscribes to the irrational belief, 'I *must* not be fired or demoted, as this would surely be evidence that I'm a complete loser.' The counsellor has now conceptualized Peter's presenting complaint in A, B and C terms.

> **Key point**
>
> When clients describe the problems that brought them to counselling in vague terms, it is important for you to operationalize these problems according to the format provided by the ABC model. When working to operationalize vague problems in ABC terms, aim for specificity. This goal can be promoted through your skilful use of questions (some of which you may choose to combine with didactic statements).

5   Develop a shared language with your clients

I (W.D.) once attended a symposium on anger where there was a lot of disagreement expressed concerning whether or not anger is a constructive emotion. This problem was compounded markedly by the fact that the delegates had differing conceptions of anger and were in fact not discussing the same emotion. In order for the delegates to have communicated constructively with one another they would have needed to agree on a shared language.

Exactly the same point holds in counselling and is especially pertinent in REBC where it is important that counsellor and client agree on using a shared language which will accurately represent key REBC concepts. Let us consider the major areas where this point becomes particularly salient.

Distinguishing between healthy and unhealthy negative emotions

As discussed briefly in the overview of REBC presented in the Introduction, REBC theory distinguishes between unhealthy negative emotions (such as anxiety, depression, guilt and anger) which are deemed to stem from irrational beliefs about negative activating events (A's) and healthy negative emotions (such as concern, sadness, remorse and annoyance) which in turn stem from rational beliefs about those same negative events.

The language of REBC here is important. For example, 'anxiety' is deemed to be an unhealthy negative emotion with 'concern' as its healthy negative counterpart. Now, as an REBC counsellor you need to know such REBC terminology, but you also need to be aware that your clients may use such words in different ways. Given this, you have two options. First, you can teach your clients the REBC terminology. Thus, in our example you can teach the REBC view on the differences between anxiety or concern. Secondly, you can use your clients' own words to reflect these differences. If you do the latter, it is important to ensure that the words your clients use actually do reflect accurately the differences between these two types of negative emotions. These differences do not only concern the different beliefs involved. As I (W.D.) have pointed out elsewhere, a healthy negative emotion leads to a different set of cognitive consequences and action tendencies from its corresponding unhealthy emotion (Dryden, 1994a, 1995a). As such, when helping your clients to understand the differences between healthy and unhealthy negative emotions, you can refer to the associated differences in beliefs, cognitive consequences and action tendencies.

Particular difficulties with certain REBC concepts

One way to look at the concepts employed in REBC is to view them as A's which are open to misinterpretation. Thus, when you use a concept such as 'rational' with your clients, be aware that when they hear this word at A, they are likely to bring to it their own way of using the word which may well reflect a different concept. As such, you may be using the same word, but be discussing two different concepts. For example, the term 'rational' in REBC means 'flexible, realistic, logical and self-helping', but a client may understand the word to mean 'cold, unfeeling and robot-like'. Unless you understand how your individual client is using the concept, then you will experience frustration as she resists accepting what you consider to be a really useful and healthy idea.

Consequently, we suggest that when you use rational concepts that are open to misinterpretation you explain what you mean *and* emphasize what you do not mean. Here is an example:

> Now, one of the goals of REBC is to help you to think rationally. By this I mean holding beliefs that are flexible, realistic, sensible and which will help you to live a happier life. I do not mean that I am

going to try to get you to think like a computer and be cold and unfeeling. Far from it. Rational thinking won't rob you of your emotions, even your intense ones. However, it will encourage you to experience healthy emotions much of the time and help you to minimize experiencing emotions that are unhealthy.

Let us now consider another important rational concept that clients tend to misconstrue: acceptance.

Acceptance

The concept of acceptance in REBC is used in two contexts: (i) accepting grim reality and (ii) accepting oneself – and others – as fallible human beings. Let us take each of these contexts in turn.

Accepting grim reality   When REBC counsellors urge their clients to accept grim reality, they mean the following.

1   Acknowledge that what happened was grim.
2   Acknowledge that unfortunately all the conditions were in place for the grim event to happen.
3   Determine whether or not you can change the grim situation.
4   If you can change it, do so.
5   If you cannot change it, feel healthily negative (but not needlessly disturbed) about it and make as constructive an adjustment as you can. In addition, if you can, involve yourself in meaningful pursuits. This will help you not to dwell on the unchangeable grim reality. However, do not expect to forget about it.

However, when some clients hear their REBC counsellors urging them to accept grim reality, they think that they are being asked to do one or more of the following:

1   Resign yourself to the situation.
2   Be indifferent to the situation.
3   Forget about the situation.

It is hardly surprising that clients who conceptualize the term 'acceptance' in this way will not respond favourably when invited to accept grim reality by their REBC counsellor.

Self-acceptance   When REBC counsellors urge their clients to accept themselves as fallible human beings for their wrongdoings, for example, they mean the following.

1 You are a unique, ongoing, everchanging human being who defies a single global rating.
2 You are fallible, which means that you are, by nature, prone to do the wrong thing at times.
3 You need to take responsibility for your wrongdoings.
4 When you don't blame yourself, you can reflect on the experience, understand why you acted in the way that you did and resolve to change your behaviour in the future.
5 You can make any suitable reparations.

However, when some clients hear their REBC counsellors urging them to accept themselves for their wrongdoings, they hear one or more of the following messages.

1 What you did can be condoned or excused.
2 You do not have to take responsibility for what you did.
3 You will have to resign yourself to the fact that you cannot change.

Again, we think it is clear why such clients will resist the invitation to work towards self-acceptance.

Thus, when encouraging a client to accept grim reality or to accept herself as a fallible human being, it is very important that you spell out exactly what you mean by these concepts, elicit her understanding of the terms and highlight the differences between the two conceptualizations. Then decide between the two of you whether to use the term 'acceptance' as it is employed in REBC theory or a term that your client prefers and which means the same thing to her as 'acceptance' means to you.

Key point

Develop a shared language with your clients, especially when using key REBC concepts. If you do so, you will work more profitably together than if you do not.

6   Develop and maintain the reflection process

In one of the Marx Brothers films, Groucho stands back from the action, which stops, and talks directly to the audience about what has been going on. This happens several times in a memorable sequence. What Groucho is doing here is reflecting on what has just occurred. We suggest that this process of standing back from the action and commenting on it can also occur in REBC to the benefit of both counsellor and client. Dryden and Feltham (1994) state that 'the reflection process is what we call the process when counsellor and client agree to discuss their rational observations of the counselling process. This involves a "stepping back" to gain perspective on the relationship and how well it is serving the interests of the client' (p. 7).

Establishing the reflection process

In REBC, it is your responsibility as counsellor to establish the reflection process, and it is best if you can do this early in the counselling process. Her is an example of how to do this.

Counsellor: I see us working together as a team with you having particular expertise on your own problems and with me having particular
expertise in one approach to helping you understand how these
problems have developed and how you can go about overcoming
them. Does that make sense?

Client: Yes, it does.

Counsellor: Now it is very important for us to let the other know if there
are problems in the workings of this team. For example, you may
think that I'm going too fast for you or I might think that you are
agreeing with me to gain my approval. Can you see that something
like this may happen?

Client: Yes, that's possible.

Counsellor: Given that this is possible, we need a way to step back as it
were from the action and invite the other person to reflect on the source
of the problem. It's a bit like taking time out. Let me give you an
example. Suppose I am explaining something to you and you are
nodding in agreement, but I get the impression that you aren't really
agreeing with me, I might say something like: 'Can we stop there for a

moment and stand back from the action? I need to check something out with you.' I'll then share my impression with you and we can discuss whether what I've observed has any validity. If it has, we'll then discuss the point and if I'm wrong then at least I've had an opportunity to test out my hunch with you. Do you see what I'm saying?

Client: Yes, I do. You want us to indicate to one another when we need to discuss some aspect of the therapy that needs discussing.

Counsellor: Right. Do you think that's a good idea?

Client: I do, but it'll seem strange at first.

Counsellor: That's right. It'll seem strange because we aren't used to doing that in everyday conversation. Now, if there's something that you want to discuss, how will you call time-out?

Client: Let's see . . . I could say something like: 'Let's stand back for a moment'.

Counsellor: That sounds good. So let's agree that we'll both do that if we need to do so at any time during our sessions. OK?

Client: OK.

Counsellor: In addition, there will be more formal opportunities to give each other feedback, such as at the end of a session or at regular progress reviews, but that doesn't preclude either of us 'stepping back' during a session.

Eliciting feedback at the end of a session

As the last counsellor response above shows, there are two opportunities for counsellor and client to make more formal use of the reflection process. Since we will discuss progress reviews in point 17, we will concentrate here on eliciting and giving feedback at the end of the session.

Beck et al. (1979) have written on the importance of eliciting feedback at the end of cognitive therapy sessions. They argue that doing so enables the client to experience that her views are being taken seriously and that she is a full partner in a collaborative enterprise. We note that many REBC counsellors do not routinely ask for client feedback at the end of counselling sessions and we think that they can gain much from doing so.

Standard questions you can ask your client at the end of a session

We will now list some standard questions that you can ask your client at the end of a session and discuss the value of such questions.

• What have you found (most) helpful about this session?

Discovering what your client has found helpful about counselling sessions can help you capitalize on such curative factors in future sessions. There is one major exception to this principle: what your client finds helpful may in the long term be countertherapeutic for her. In such a case you would not seek to offer more of this factor.

- What have you found unhelpful (or least helpful) about this session?

Clients generally find answering this question difficult at least at the beginning of counselling, and with a given client you may have to stress the importance of her giving a response if you are to minimize unhelpful factors. As with the previous question, you need to evaluate your client's response carefully since you may not wish to refrain from doing something that you consider helpful just because your client finds it unhelpful. Before abandoning its use you may need to explain what you are doing and why you are doing it and ask for suggestions concerning how you might do it differently. After doing all this, if your client still finds it unhelpful stop using it; otherwise you will threaten the therapeutic alliance to the detriment of your client's well-being.

- How helpful or unhelpful did you find . . . ?

Here you are making a specific enquiry about a specific intervention that you made (for example, self-disclosure) or a more general style of practising counselling (for example, Socratic questioning). Your client's responses will help you to determine whether you will make greater or lesser use of the intervention or style or, indeed, abandon it altogether.

Giving feedback to the client at the end of a session

Sometimes your client will ask you for feedback at the end of a session. We suggest that you give it if it is brief and non-contentious. If you can respond to a simple client question or offer an opinion on something about the REBC counselling process that does not need exploration then we suggest that you do so.

However, if your client asks for feedback that is likely to lead to a discussion lasting more than two minutes or that touches on a contentious issue then we recommend that you postpone the issue until the next session. Thus, you might say something like: 'You raise an important issue to which I will respond, but it will take longer than the few moments that we have left. I suggest that we begin the next session by looking at it. Can we agree to do that?'

Make a note of the issue and remind yourself to raise it for discussion at the beginning of the next session. Failure to do so is bad practice.

Key point

Establish the reflection process early on in REBC counselling, use it throughout the counselling process as a way of raising and dealing with significant issues with clients and encourage them to do the same. Use other, more formal opportunities to reflect with clients about the progress of counselling (such as at the end of counselling sessions).

II Improving Your REBC Skills in Counselling Sessions

7 Keep on track in using the counselling sequence

The REBC counselling sequence outlines 13 important steps that a counsellor needs to follow in order to do a thorough job of helping a client to deal with a given problem (see Dryden, 1990, for an extended discussion of this sequence). The framework provided by the counselling sequence will assist you in structuring individual counselling sessions as well as the entire counselling process. By employing the counselling sequence you help to ensure that you, as counsellor, have conducted an adequate assessment, taught the B–C connection, disputed thoroughly, and engaged in other relevant counsellor tasks. When you are consistent in your use of the counselling sequence, you can make counselling a much more understandable experience for your clients. Also, your use of the counselling sequence can serve to teach your clients how to utilize a structured approach to emotional problem-solving. In the section that follows, we review some commonly encountered obstacles to keeping on track with the counselling sequence, and provide some suggestions for dealing with them. We then discuss circumstances in which it would be appropriate to change course with respect to your use of the counselling sequence.

Common obstacles to keeping on track with the counselling sequence

Clients who provide lengthy descriptions of A or C

Ellis (1991a) has noted that many clients, particularly those with prior experience in psychoanalysis, 'love to describe the unfortunate Activating Events of their lives in long and gory detail' (p. 6). Other clients may be prone to talk compulsively about the negative feelings (C's) that they are experiencing. While doing so may have a cathartic effect that temporarily helps these clients to feel better, it can sidetrack counsellors from efficiently conducting the assessment and intervention tasks that are part and parcel of the counselling sequence. With clients who provide lengthy descriptions of A, attempt to interrupt tactfully and re-establish a specific problem focus. This can be accomplished by making the following sort of statement: 'I think you're probably giving me more background information than I require in order to be of help to you. Tell me what it was about this situation that you were most upset about.' With clients who dwell compulsively on their negative feelings, you can say the following: 'I can see that you're really feeling a lot of emotional distress. If we work together, I think we can develop some ways for you to change some of the negative feelings you're describing. Would you like to do this?' Here, it is important to note that some clients may enter counselling with preconceived notions that they will get better if they fully vent their upsets in sessions. Be alert to the possibility that your client may subscribe to this notion. If this is the case, allow time to discuss with your client the nature of REBC treatment.

Client reluctance to disclose a problem

Some clients will be reluctant to disclose an emotional problem because they feel ashamed that they have the problem. If your client speaks about a negative activating event but does not admit to having an emotional problem about the A you are discussing, assess for the presence of shame. This can be accomplished by posing the following sort of question to your client: 'If you actually *did* have an emotional problem about the circumstances we've been discussing, how would you then feel?' If your assessment reveals the presence of shame, attempt to come to an agreement with your client to target this feeling for change before returning to the original problem your client may have had in mind.

Clients who jump from problem to problem

If your client jumps from problem to problem during counselling sessions, it will of course be difficult to implement the steps comprising the counselling sequence. Therefore, it is important to explain to your client that your time together will yield better results if the two of you collaboratively work on one problem at a time. After providing this explanation, ask your client to pick a problem to focus on that she regards as most relevant or most important. Also note that setting an agenda at the start of the session concerning what you and your client will discuss during that particular session can also help to mitigate this problem.

Some clients may jump from topic to topic within counselling sessions because of anxiety or conditions such as attention deficit disorder or a manic state. If you suspect that your client's lack of focus stems from anxiety, conduct an assessment to determine whether this is so and what your client is feeling anxious about. Then, attempt to attain agreement to target this anxiety as a problem to work on. If you suspect that your client has one of the other conditions mentioned above, it may be appropriate to discuss tactfully psychiatric referral for possible psychopharmacological treatment.

Insufficient time to discuss homework assignments

In keeping with the counselling sequence, it is desirable to allow sufficient time within counselling sessions to collaborate with clients on the design of relevant homework assignments. Often, however, novice counsellors save this activity for the very end of a session and find that they lack the time to discuss adequately the what, where, when and how of homework assignments. Try to structure your sessions so that they almost always include discussion of and agreement upon a homework assignment, as your consistency in doing so will help to communicate to your clients that such assignments are an integral part of the counselling process. Make a point of checking clients' homework assignments when they return for the next session, as this also underscores the importance of homework assignments and provides you with the opportunity to conduct trouble-shooting. (See points 22 and 26 for a more detailed discussion of negotiating and checking homework assignments.)

When to change course with the counselling sequence

While it is desirable to stay with the REBC counselling sequence until your client has reached coping criteria on the particular problem that has been targeted for change, there are circumstances where it is appropriate to deviate from the sequence in order to deal with another client problem.

After you have agreed upon and started working on a target problem with your client, for example, you may find that she develops another problem that becomes more pressing. As an example, a client may experience a major negative activating event (such as serious marital discord, job loss, or diagnosis of cancer) that was not at issue when counselling began. If your client has an emotional problem about this new negative A that pervasively affects her functioning and makes it difficult to concentrate efforts (both inside and outside of sessions) on the original target problems, then it can make good clinical sense to change tack and deal with this new problem. If you fail to do so, it may communicate to your client that you care more about following your own agenda than you do about her welfare. Before changing tack make sure your client agrees that this is appropriate, and try to remain on track with the treatment sequence until progress has been made in dealing with the new emotional problem.

You will also find that clients sometimes develop emotional problems concerning their counsellor and the counselling process. Young (1994) has noted, for instance, that clients with personality disorders will often bring to bear on the therapeutic relationship the same sorts of interpersonal problems they tend to experience with others outside of counselling. Thus, certain clients may make themselves quite angry about the fact that, in their perception, their counsellor has treated them inconsiderately or unfairly. Other clients may make themselves anxious and/or depressed about how well (or poorly) they see themselves doing in counselling. When you see that your client has an emotional problem about you or about some aspect of the counselling process that is interfering with her progress in counselling, suggest that the two of you turn attention to dealing with this problem. After some progress has been made in working on this new problem (such that it no longer poses a significant threat to your client's progress), work can resume on the problem originally targeted for change. Remember that the steps comprising the counselling sequence are just as relevant to dealing with your client's problems about counselling as they are to dealing with the other types of emotional problems your client may present. See point 18 for additional material related to clients' emotional problems about counselling.

> **Key point**
>
> It is important to keep on track in using the counselling sequence, as this will facilitate effective treatment and model to your clients a structured approach for conducting emotional problem-solving. It can be appropriate to deviate temporarily from the treatment sequence when your client develops a new emotional problem that interferes with work on the problem originally targeted for change.

8 Take care in assessing the complexities of A

It does not take beginning REBC counsellors long to discover that A in the ABC model stands for activating event. It also does not take them long to appreciate the REBC point that A's contribute to clients' unhealthy negative feelings, but do not cause these reactions. However, it does take trainees quite a long time to appreciate the complexities of A, and even longer to assess these complexities accurately.

Let us briefly consider the complexities of A before considering in detail one way that you can assess difficult-to-identity A's.

The complexities of A

A's can be literally anything that triggers a person's rational or irrational beliefs which are at the core of his emotional experience. When they do trigger the person's beliefs, these A's are known as critical A's (Dryden, 1995a).

Critical A's can be actual or inferred, external or internal, or occur in the present, past or future. If we combine these dimensions, you will see the range of A's that may serve to trigger a client's irrational beliefs.

- Actual present, external event.
- Actual past, external event.

- Actual future, external event.
- Inference of present, external event.
- Inference of past, external event.
- Inference of future, external event.
- Actual present, internal event.
- Actual past, internal event.
- Actual future, internal event.
- Inference of present, internal event.
- Inference of past, internal event.
- Inference of future, internal event.

When it is not clear what the critical A is in your client's emotional episode, how can you identify it?

Identifying the critical A

I (W.D.) have outlined 12 ways that you can identify your client's difficult-to-identify critical A (Dryden, 1995a). Space obviously precludes consideration of all 12 methods, so we will consider only one here: inference chaining.

Inference chaining

Inference chaining is a method designed to identify your client's critical A by recognizing that inferences are often chained together and that one of these links in the inferential chain serves to trigger the client's irrational belief. Let us consider an example. Here, the counsellor knows that the client has received a note from his personal tutor at college asking him to go and see her and the client is anxious about doing so. In inference chaining, it is important to keep the client's target emotion to the fore, which in this example is anxiety. Before we consider this example, we wish to make clear that the counsellor explains the use of inference chaining to the client before carrying it out. Otherwise clients may react as if they are receiving 'the third degree'.

Counsellor: So, Terry, what were you anxious about? All the note said was that your tutor wanted to see you.
Client: I'm sure she wants to see me because I've done something wrong. [*In inference chaining it is important that you do not question the empirical status of any of the inferences that your client discloses – in other words, refrain from disputing these inferences. If you do so, you will not identify his*

critical A. Instead, assume temporarily that your client's inferences are correct and use them to go further along the inference chain.]

Counsellor: Let's assume that for the moment. What would be anxiety-provoking about her seeing you because you've done something wrong?

[*In this intervention, the counsellor keeps the target emotion, anxiety, to the fore.*]

Client: Well, she will be angry with me.

Counsellor: And if she's angry, what would be anxiety-provoking about her being angry with you?

Client: Well, if she is angry with me, she'll criticize me.

Counsellor: And if she criticizes you, what would that mean?

[*Another way of exploring inference chains is to ask for the meaning of the stated inference.*]

Client: That would mean that she'll remember my name.

Counsellor: And if she does, what would be scary about her remembering your name?

Client: She won't give me a good reference.

Counsellor: And if she doesn't give you a good reference, what would be scary about that in your mind?

Client: It will damage my career.

Counsellor: And if your career is damaged . . .

[*Yet another way of exploring an inference chain is to ask the client to complete an unfinished sentence, as the counsellor does in this response.*]

Client: Oh, my God! That would be terrible.

[*When a client spontaneously comes up with an irrational belief, this is one sign that you have identified a critical A, but you still need to check this out.*]

Counsellor: What would be terrible about that?

Client: It just would be. It would be awful if my career was damaged before it's really under way.

[*When a client repeats himself in a way that this client did, this is another sign that you have probably identified a critical A in that the client fails to provide another inference. However, since it is possible that the critical A may be an inference that the client has already given you, you should now review the chain with your client and ask him to select the inference that best explains what he was most anxious about.*]

Counsellor: OK. I am going to feed back what you've told me and as I do so I want you to select the element that you were most anxious about in the situation with your tutor. Choose the one that best explains what you were most anxious about at the time, even though it may sound ridiculous now. OK?

Client: OK.

Counsellor: Right, you mentioned the following:

The note which said that your tutor wanted to see you.
The fact that you'd done something wrong.
Your tutor being angry with you.
Your tutor criticizing you.
Your tutor remembering your name.
Your tutor not giving you a good reference.

Your career being damaged as a result of not having a good
reference from your tutor.
Now, which element do you think best explains what you were
anxious about at the time?
Client: The last one – the fact that not getting a good reference will
damage my career.

From this inference chain and review, it is clear that the client's
critical A concerns his career being damaged. This will then serve
as the A in this client's ABC and the counsellor will then help the
client to articulate his irrational beliefs about this A.

After the counsellor has helped the client to challenge his
irrational beliefs and has achieved a fair measure of belief change,
the counsellor can then invite the client to consider the empirical
status of the inferences he made in this episode. Generally
speaking, clients are more likely to question successfully their
distorted inferences when they are thinking rationally than when
they are thinking irrationally.

Readers interested in learning other methods for identifying the
critical A are advised to consult Dryden (1995a).

Key point

Dealing with clients' A's can be a difficult process given the
complexities of activating events. Take care when assessing
clients' difficult-to-identify A's and use such methods as
inference chaining when doing so.

---

9 Teach and re-teach the ABC of REBC

One of the tasks fundamental to your role as counsellor is to teach
(and re-teach) your clients the ABC of REBC. Clients who fail to
grasp the ABC model may continue to blame their emotional
upsets on the unfortunate activating events in their lives and may
fail to understand why you are attempting to dispute their
irrational beliefs within sessions. This state of affairs, of course,
does not lend itself to conducting effective REBC treatment.

Clients who understand the ABC model will have at their disposal a useful tool for conceptualizing the origins of their emotional distress. Furthermore, clients who grasp the B–C connection will be more likely to focus efforts on modifying their irrational beliefs.

In teaching the ABC model to your clients, you will want to be sure that they acquire the three main insights of REBC (Ellis, 1984).

1 Unhealthy negative emotions are not caused by negative activating events, but are largely determined by the irrational beliefs that individuals bring to bear upon those events.
2 Individuals remain disturbed by re-indoctrinating themselves in the present with their irrational beliefs.
3 The process of challenging and changing the irrational beliefs that underpin emotional disturbance involves *consistent* work and practice.

We will now review a number of points germane to teaching and re-teaching your clients the ABC of REBC.

Expose your client to the ABC model at an early point in the counselling process.

As you engage in the assessment tasks that are part of the counselling sequence, you will be providing your client with her first exposure to the ABC model. Take steps to summarize the results of your assessment activities for your client, so that she can begin to understand the REBC approach to problem conceptualization. Attempt to employ relevant REBC terminology as you provide this summary, in order to teach your client the meaning of terms such as activating event, rational and irrational belief, and emotional consequences. You may opt to write out the ABC of your client's emotional problem on a sheet of paper (clearly delineating the relationships between activating events, beliefs and emotional consequences) in order to facilitate the teaching process. Here, it is noted that some clients will learn more quickly when a verbal presentation is supplemented with a visual presentation.

Check your client's understanding of your assessment summary

After summarizing for your client the results of your ABC assessment, check to make sure she understands what you are talking about. This can be accomplished with the following sort of statement: 'I've just described a way of understanding the origin of the upsets you've been experiencing. In your own words, can you summarize for me what you've understood me to be saying?' If your client's response reveals misunderstandings, these can be corrected at this point.

Use language consistent with the ABC model

Novice REBC counsellors will sometimes employ language with their clients in a way that serves to reinforce the idea that A causes C. This, of course, runs counter to the ABC model, which holds that B largely determines the emotional C a person will experience in response to a negative A.

The most frequent sort of error that beginning counsellors make in this regard is to pose the following sort of question after a client has described a negative A: 'How did that *make you* feel?' A better question to ask when attempting to assess an emotional C is 'How did you feel about that?'

Offer corrections when clients make an A–C connection

Even after clients have been directly taught the ABC model and have demonstrated understanding of the B–C connection, they will still sometimes make statements that seem to indicate that they subscribe to the view that negative activating events cause their emotional problems. A given client, for example, may state 'When I found out I didn't get the promotion at work, it made me feel depressed.' When presented with a statement such as this, the counsellor can respond by saying, 'Do you mean that *it* depressed you, or that you depressed yourself *about* it?' This type of response can serve to reinforce the B–C connection in the client's mind. Note, however, that as counsellor you do not want to use this sort of statement in an automatic fashion each time a client verbalizes an A–C connection. Some clients will feel exasperated and may even become angry if they think that you are correcting their manner of speaking all of the time.

Encourage clients to analyse their upsets with the ABC model independently

After initially teaching clients the ABC model with respect to the first problem targeted for change within counselling, encourage them to conduct their own ABC analysis with respect to subsequent emotional problems that become a focus of treatment. Within sessions, this can be prompted by making the following sort of statement: 'We've been discussing the upset you experience when your husband criticizes you. How would you describe this problem with the ABC model?'

Clients can also be encouraged to use REBC homework sheets between sessions to break their emotional problems down into their A, B and C components. Point 24 in this book provides further details of this type of assignment.

Teach the nuances of the ABC model

After your client acquires a basic understanding of the ABC model, you can begin to teach him explicitly about some of the nuances and subtleties of this model. This can increase his ability to function as his own counsellor, and may also serve to maintain his interest in the counselling process. To cite an example, after your client understands how to conceptualize primary problems with the ABC sequence, you can teach him how to use the sequence to recognize, analyse and deal with secondary emotional problems. As another example of 'advanced material' that may prove helpful for your client to acquire, you can teach him how to broaden his conceptualization of A. It will, for instance, be useful for him to see that A does not always have to be an event that has already actually occurred; it can also be an anticipated negative *future* event. Finally, some clients may benefit from being taught about the complex ways in which A's, B's, and C's may interact (Ellis, 1991b). In particular, you may want certain of your clients to see that their irrational beliefs may negatively distort their inferences at A. In terms of introducing 'advanced' material to your clients, exercise your judgement with respect to 'how much' and 'how fast'. Too much at once may serve to confuse your client and divert him from solidifying his knowledge about the basic ABC.

**Encourage clients to utilize REBC
psychoeducational materials**

A good number of excellent REBC self-help books and audio tapes are available for clients to use. Suggesting that clients obtain and use REBC psychoeducational materials of relevance to their emotional problems represents an additional way of reinforcing their learning of the ABC model and the very important B–C connection.

Key point

Make efforts to teach clients how to conceptualize their emotional problems with the ABC model early on in the counselling process, and reinforce this teaching at various appropriate points as counselling proceeds. In particular, encourage clients to utilize the ABC independently as a means for understanding and remediating their emotional problems. Clients who acquire facility in using the ABC model will ultimately be in a better position to act as their own counsellors.

---

10 Check your clients' understanding of your teaching points

Ellis (1973, p. 15) has indicated that his role as counsellor in large part 'consists of involved, concerned, vigorous *teaching*'. REBC can indeed be characterized as a psychoeducational approach to counselling, as it seeks to teach clients actively how to resolve their emotional problems independently. Thus, as you do REBC with your clients, it makes good sense to check their understanding of the many important teaching points you will be trying to convey. While conducting such checking may at times seem awkward (particularly if you are unaccustomed to doing it), failure to do so can result in counselling that is less efficient and effective. A good number of clients will often fail to let you know when they do not know what you are talking about, so it is important for you, as an active–directive counsellor, to take the lead in avoiding misunderstandings.

Guidelines for checking client understanding

When an important teaching point is first presented to clients within counselling, a simple question can usually be used to check clients' understanding of it: 'Can you tell me in your own words what you've just understood me to be saying?' If you are concerned that your clients will think you are questioning their intelligence (and perhaps become angry at you) when you make such an inquiry, you can use this alternative: 'I want to be sure that I've expressed myself clearly on this point. Can you recap for me what I've just been saying?' Note, however, that you can be alert to the possibility that some clients may experience anger or hurt if they believe that you are questioning their intelligence, and that you can directly provide clarification as to the reason for your checking questions.

If clients appear to hesitate or are unable to respond when you ask them a checking question, and this appears to be due to a lack of understanding, attempt to offer clarification of your teaching point. Then, re-check to be sure they are now clear on your point.

Watch for non-verbal cues to non-understanding

While a good number of clients will neglect to tell you verbally that they do not understand what you are talking about, they will probably inadvertently provide you with a number of non-verbal cues to their lack of comprehension. W.D. has identified the following two behaviours as signs that a client does not understand what the counsellor is saying (Dryden, 1991).

1 *The glazed look.* Here, the client displays a glazed expression, often accompanied by a fixed smile.
2 *The automatic head nod.* Here clients nod knowingly as if they understand their counsellor's meaning.

In addition, J.Y. has noted that certain clients engage in 'anxious' behaviours when they are not following a point their counsellor is trying to make. Such behaviours include nail biting, pulling on one's lip, dropping eye contact, and restlessly shifting in one's seat. If you observe any of these behaviours in your client while you are trying to convey a point, it may be wise to pause and employ a checking question.

Be alert to client embarrassment

As noted above, clients will sometimes fail to tell you that they do not understand a point you have been trying to make. Sometimes this is because they experience embarrassment (in relation to their lack of comprehension) stemming from the following sort of irrational belief: 'I *must* not reveal to my counsellor that I don't understand a word she's said. If I ask her to repeat herself, she'll think that I'm a complete idiot – and she'll be right!' Likewise, some clients will experience embarrassment when you ask them a checking question and, because of lack of understanding, they are unable to respond adequately. If you suspect that your client feels embarrassed when unable to feed back to you your teaching point, assess whether this is the case and deal with it by (a) stating that many people have some trouble grasping new material upon its first presentation, and (b) showing your client the irrational belief that underpins her feeling of embarrassment and working with her to challenge it.

Follow-up on important teaching points in subsequent sessions

If during a given session you present a teaching point to your client that you consider particularly important, you can choose to follow-up on your client's understanding of that point in a subsequent session. As an example, you might pose the following sort of question to your client near the start of a new session: 'Last week when we met, I described to you a particular model for understanding where your anxiety comes from. Can you tell me what you recall about that?' Checking client understanding across sessions in this manner can serve to underscore for your client the importance of particular points that you wish her to learn. In addition, it can help to contribute to continuity between sessions.

Junctures at which to check client understanding

The following is a list of some key junctures at which it may be wise to check your client's understanding of your teaching points.

1 When discussing the respective tasks of counsellor and client within REBC.
2 When describing the REBC approach to emotional problem-solving.
3 When describing the ABC model and the importance of the B–C connection.
4 After going through a dispute of a particular irrational belief that your client subscribes to.
5 When providing a rationale for the concept of homework assignments in general, or when providing a rationale for a specific homework assignment that you have suggested to your client.

Key point

Since REBC is a psychoeducational approach to counselling, it is a good idea to check client understanding of the various teaching points you will be trying to convey. This can usually be accomplished by asking your clients to feed back to you (in their own words) what you have just been saying. Failure to check client understanding of your teaching points can result in counselling that is less efficient and effective.

---

11   Look out for and deal with the two major types of disturbance

Ellis (1979a, 1980a) has made the observation that many psychological problems can be viewed as falling into two major categories: ego disturbance and discomfort disturbance. Ego disturbance arises when human beings create absolutistic conditions for 'self-worth', and then engage in global negative self-rating when these self-created conditions are not met. Discomfort disturbance relates to absolutistic demands for comfort and comfortable life conditions. When these demands are not met, the individual subscribing to them experiences disturbance. The healthy alternative to ego disturbance is unconditional self-acceptance, which involves acknowledging one's fallibility while refusing to apply a single, all-encompassing rating to one's self. The healthy alternative to discomfort disturbance involves a philosophy of high frustration or discomfort tolerance, which can facilitate attainment of valued goals and contribute to long-range happiness. In your work with clients, it is important to determine whether one or both of these broad categories of disturbance are implicated in your clients' problems. In the two sections that follow, we review (using case examples) some of the more subtle ways that ego disturbance and discomfort disturbance may manifest themselves.

Subtle manifestations of ego disturbance

Ego disturbance will often be relatively easy to identify in your work with clients, as when they experience anxiety about the possibility of receiving negative judgements from other people (which they would then accept as 'proof' of their lack of worth), guilt in relation to some negative act they believe they have committed, or depression involving self-damnation. Sometimes, however, ego disturbance will manifest itself in more subtle ways that are less readily identified.

Ego disturbance and anger

Ego disturbance can sometimes be involved in clients' angry upsets. To cite an example, a given client may indicate to you that he is very angry at his boss for passing him over for a significant promotion at work. At first glance, this emotional problem (the client's anger) may seem to stem from the following sort of irrational belief: 'My boss *should* have recognized my talents and awarded me this promotion! He's a totally damnable human being for not doing so!' However, if you work with the client to identify what for him is the most disturbing aspect of being passed over for promotion (as you would do in inference chaining, described in point 8), you may discover that he is really worried about the possibility that his co-workers will regard him as incompetent and laugh behind his back when they learn that he did not receive the promotion. As your client has a self-created need for the approval of others as a condition for ascribing worth to himself, these negative judgements would represent a threat to 'self-esteem' for your client. Thus, his anger towards his boss actually represents a manifestation of ego disturbance.

Ego disturbance masquerading as discomfort disturbance

Clients will sometimes present themselves for counselling because they are procrastinating on important tasks. Initially, as counsellor, you may be tempted to assume that such a problem stems from discomfort disturbance: your client is avoiding the task in question because the discomfort involved in completing it is 'intolerable'. However, it is sometimes the case that individuals avoid a task because they fear that poor performance on it will 'prove' that they are unworthy human beings. In instances such as this, dealing with the underlying self-rating issues can facilitate progress on the avoided task.

Subtle manifestations of discomfort disturbance

Ellis (1979a, 1980a) has indicated that although clients' ego disturbance may manifest itself in rather obvious and dramatic ways, discomfort disturbance, while less dramatic, can significantly interfere with clients' happiness and satisfaction in life. Like ego disturbance, discomfort disturbance can sometimes be involved in clients' emotional problems in subtle ways.

Discomfort disturbance masquerading as ego disturbance

In your work as a counsellor, you may sometimes encounter a client who is procrastinating on a task that involves advance preparation for some sort of performance before an audience (preparing a presentation for a corporation's board of directors, for example). Given that a performance in front of others is involved, you might first assume that your client is avoiding doing his advance work because of the ego anxiety he experiences whenever he thinks about the possibility of receiving disapproval from his future audience. This, however, is not necessarily the case. Your client may be engaging in task avoidance because in reality he subscribes to the irrational belief: 'Preparation for this performance *should* be easier than it is! It's too hard, and I can't stand it!' Treating your client's problem as ego disturbance in this scenario would be ineffectual, whereas helping him to see and challenge the irrational beliefs under-pinning his discomfort disturbance will probably facilitate task completion.

Discomfort disturbance and client non-compliance

It is not uncommon to encounter clients who 'forgot' or 'didn't have time' to complete their counselling homework. When non-compliance with homework assignments appears habitual, it is worthwhile trying to explore with your client why this is occur-ring. Such exploration will sometimes reveal that your client has irrational beliefs about the counselling process in general and about homework assignments in particular that contribute to avoidance of homework tasks. These beliefs can take the following forms: 'It *should* be easier to change in counselling than it is! I *shouldn't* have to devote so much time and energy between sessions to trying to get better! I *can't tolerate* all of this hard work!' It is important to show your client how these beliefs interfere with his progress in counselling, and to help him challenge and replace them.

A note on distinguishing between ego disturbance and discomfort disturbance

Within REBC, counsellors often use a client's emotional and behavioural C's as a basis for forming initial hypotheses about operative irrational beliefs. Thus, with a given client who experi-ences angry feelings toward another person, you might at first consider that other-directed absolutistic demands are at the root of your client's anger. Using client C's as a basis for forming clinical hypotheses can, however, be misleading, as suggested by the preceding discussions on subtle manifestations of ego dis-turbance and discomfort disturbance. In addition to using client C's for forming your hunches about operative irrational beliefs, you can also utilize client A's as a basis for forming your clinical hypotheses. If you know specifically what it is your client is upsetting himself about, you can then be more sure as to the form of his irrational beliefs and the type of disturbance he is experiencing. We again refer you back to point 8, which discussed inference chaining, for further information on this issue.

Key point

Many of the emotional problems that clients present in counselling can be subsumed under the two categories of ego disturbance and discomfort disturbance. By remaining alert to the possibility that a given client may have one or both of these types of disturbance, you can be more confident that you are doing an accurate and comprehensive job of assessing your client's problem. Remember, however, that ego disturbance and discomfort disturbance can sometimes manifest themselves in subtle ways. You can help yourself to distinguish between them by using your clients' A's, as well as their C's, as a basis for forming your hypotheses as to their operative irrational beliefs.

---

12 Be comprehensive in your disputing

After you have assessed the irrational beliefs underpinning your client's disturbance (and have made sure that she understands the B–C connection), you will want to work on disputing these beliefs in a comprehensive manner. Comprehensive disputing means that you are disputing your client's irrational beliefs in a thoroughgoing and complete fashion, such that your client will more readily surrender these beliefs in favour of more rational, helpful ones (see point 16).

DiGiuseppe (1991) has presented a useful model for conducting comprehensive disputing in an organized manner. He presents four categories of variables (relevant to the disputing process) which you, as counsellor, can manipulate within sessions to increase the likelihood that your disputing activities will be complete and effective. These four categories are:

1   the *type* of disputing argument used;
2   the *style* of the disputing argument;
3   the *level of abstraction* of the irrational beliefs targeted for disputing;
4   the irrational belief *processes* targeted for disputing.

We will briefly describe each of these variables and then present some caveats to bear in mind as you attempt to implement comprehensive disputing with your clients.

Type of disputing argument

Irrational beliefs tend to be illogical, anti-empirical and self-defeating (meaning that they create significant upsets and often contribute to obstacles to goal attainment). As such, they can be challenged with logical, empirical and pragmatic disputing arguments.

Logical disputing arguments

With this type of disputing argument, your goal is to help your client understand why her irrational belief is illogical. Frequently this involves showing your client that just because she *prefers* that conditions be a particular way, it is an illogical *non sequitur* for her to conclude that these conditions absolutely *must* exist. That which is preferable does not *have to* be, and REBC theory holds that human beings are more likely to disturb themselves when they conclude otherwise.

Empirical disputing arguments

This type of disputing argument attempts to demonstrate that absolutistic demands (with their associated derivatives of awful-izing, negative person-rating and I-can't-stand-it-itis) are almost always inconsistent with empirically determined reality. Empirical disputing involves the use of questions which ask your client to provide evidence in support of her irrational beliefs. Thus, for example, you might ask your client 'Where is the evidence that you *must* have your boyfriend's love, and that if you don't you're a worthless person?' You can show your client that any 'evidence' she cites does not in reality constitute sound support of her belief.

Pragmatic disputing arguments

Here, your goal is to bring to your client's attention the pragmatic consequences of subscribing to irrational beliefs. This involves using questions such as, 'Where is believing that you *have to* succeed going to get you, other than winding up feeling anxious and depressed?' Essentially, you are underscoring for your client the fact that advocating irrational beliefs will lead to self-defeating emotional (and behavioural) outcomes.

With reference to Kuhn's (1970) work on the factors which influence scientists to discard old theories in favour of new, alternative ones, DiGiuseppe (1991) argues that clients will be more likely to relinquish their irrational beliefs (and replace them with rational ones) when all three types of disputing arguments are used.

Style of disputing argument

At least five particular disputing styles can be identified (DiGiuseppe, 1991; Dryden and Yankura, 1993): Socratic, didactic, humorous, metaphorical and self-disclosing.

Socratic disputing style

This involves using carefully chosen questions which lead your client to think about and see for herself the illogical, empirically inconsistent and self-defeating aspects of her irrational beliefs. It is often the preferred style of REBC counsellors, as it requires clients to be active participants in the process of disputing their irrational beliefs. Also, many clients may be more inclined to surrender their irrational beliefs when they 'see for themselves' that a disputing argument is valid, as opposed to simply being told it is valid by their counsellor.

Didactic disputing style

The didactic style involves directly teaching clients the reasons why their irrational beliefs are illogical, anti-empirical and self-defeating. Typically, it will be necessary to utilize didactic explanations at various points during the counselling process, as clients will not always catch on to your teaching points with the Socratic style. Even when you attempt to use direct teaching, however, it is a good idea to check your client's understanding of the point you are trying to convey (see point 10). Also, note that it is generally good practice to employ both the Socratic and didactic styles, as too much lecturing during sessions (as with the didactic style) may prove counterproductive if your goal is to facilitate client learning.

Humorous disputing style

With some clients, it can be productive to use humorous exaggeration and other humorous techniques as a means for showing them the fatuous nature of their irrational beliefs. As an example of humorous exaggeration, Albert Ellis once responded to a client who claimed he was unable to control his overeating by stating, 'That's right! The food jumps into your mouth and forces itself down your throat! It can't resist you!' (Yankura and Dryden, 1990). Note, however, that not all clients will have a positive response to a humorous disputing style. This point will receive further discussion below.

Metaphorical disputing style

Metaphors can be used quite effectively in REBC to convey important principles and assist in the disputing process. When constructing a metaphor to use with your client, try to tailor it to her in some particular way to maximize its relevance. Thus, with an athletic client, you might construct a sports metaphor to help her overcome her low frustration tolerance about enacting homework assignments: 'It's just like body-building – you won't develop your disputing muscles if you don't exercise them.'

Self-disclosing style

With some clients, counsellor self-disclosure can represent a powerful tool for disputing irrational beliefs. We recommend that you use the coping model (as opposed to the mastery model) of self-disclosure, wherein you disclose (a) that you experienced a problem that is similar in some way to your client's problem; (b) that your personal problem stemmed from an irrational belief similar to the one your client holds; and (c) how you worked hard at challenging this belief such that you no longer have the problem. The mastery model would involve conveying that you have never experienced an emotional problem similar to your client's because you have always thought rationally about the issue at hand, or that you had the problem but managed to overcome it easily. This approach tends to accentuate the differences between counsellor and client, and in our experience it is less helpful than the coping model. As with the humorous disputing style, there are certain cautions to observe (to be discussed below) with respect to using a self-disclosing style.

Level of abstraction

Clients will typically have irrational beliefs that take a very general form (for example, 'Other people *must* always treat me with consideration and fairness') as well as increasingly specific forms ('My friends and family *must* always act considerately towards me'; 'My wife *must* have dinner ready and on the table when I get home from work'). DiGiuseppe (1991) advocates that counsellors move up and down the 'ladder of abstraction' as they dispute their client's irrational beliefs in order to help ensure that they will be able to generalize their application of REBC from one specific negative activating event to others. (This issue will receive further treatment in point 13.)

Irrational belief processes

DiGiuseppe (1991) conceptualizes irrational belief processes as consisting of the core process of demandingness, along with the derivative processes of awfulizing, negative person-rating and I-can't-stand-it-itis. You are advised not to assume that disputing efforts aimed at one irrational belief process will generalize to other irrational belief processes implicated in your client's emotional problem. It makes good clinical sense to attempt to identify and dispute all irrational belief processes that may be involved.

Caveats concerning comprehensive disputing

As you attempt to conduct comprehensive disputing with your clients, it is advisable to keep the following points in mind.

Be sure you have laid proper groundwork Make sure your clients grasp the B–C connection and understand the purpose of your disputing activities within sessions. Otherwise, they may view you as argumentative and non-supportive when you attempt to challenge their irrational beliefs.

Refrain from being overly persistent If your client fails to see the validity of a particular type of disputing argument after you have taken reasonable steps to demonstrate it, switch tack and try another type of dispute. I (J.Y.) have noted that some clients who fail to grasp and benefit from logical and empirical disputing will develop a willingness to surrender their irrational beliefs after exposure to pragmatic disputing.

Watch your pace It is certainly not necessary to attempt to accomplish complete, comprehensive disputing of a particular irrational belief within a single (or even several) counselling sessions. Individuals learn at different rates, and you do not want to present your clients with more new information than they are able to effectively assimilate.

Experiment with a variety of disputing styles You may find that a given client appears to have a better response to some disputing styles than to others. Even if, however, you see a positive response to one particular style, refrain from compulsively over-using this style. What seems to work well at one point will not necessarily work as well at other points of the counselling process.

Be judicious in your use of the humorous and self-disclosing styles Prior to utilizing these two styles, it is wise to be sure that you have established a good working relationship with your client. Be judicious in your use of a humorous style until you have some evidence that your client does indeed possess a sense of humour. Also, make sure that she understands that your humorous interventions are aimed at challenging her irrational beliefs and are not attempts to poke fun at her.

Certain clients will have a negative response to counsellor self-disclosure, even when the coping model is employed. Some clients will condemn the counsellor when any sign of 'weakness' is revealed, while others may worry that if their counsellor has had emotional problems in the past, he or she is no 'stronger' than they are and may not be able to help them in the present. As such, be cautious in your use of self-disclosure with individuals who tend to be very dependent or angrily demanding toward other people. If a client responds negatively to self-disclosure, try using other types of disputing styles.

Key point

Comprehensive disputing can help your clients to surrender their irrational beliefs in favour of more rational ones. You can conduct comprehensive disputing by manipulating a number of variables germane to the disputing process. In doing comprehensive disputing, keep these guidelines in mind:

1 make sure your clients know *why* you are disputing their beliefs;
2 refrain from being overly persistent with any particular disputing argument;
3 watch your pace;
4 experiment with a variety of disputing styles.

Be judicious in your use of humorous and self-disclosing disputing styles.

---

13 Identify and deal with your clients' core irrational beliefs

Ellis (1980b) has described efficient counselling as having the qualities of *depth-centredness* and *pervasiveness*. *Depth-centredness* refers to a focus within counselling on helping clients to identify and deal with the underlying 'causes' of their emotional and behavioural problems. *Pervasiveness* refers to the process of helping clients to deal with *many* of their problems, as opposed to focusing only upon their presenting symptoms. By helping your clients to identify and deal with their core irrational beliefs, you can help bring the qualities of depth-centredness and pervasiveness to your REBC practice.

What are core irrational beliefs?

In the earlier discussion on comprehensive disputing, we suggested that it is clinically wise to move up and down the 'ladder of abstraction' as you dispute your client's irrational beliefs. This is because clients typically subscribe to irrational beliefs that have a general form as well as increasingly specific forms. A core irrational belief can be regarded as a very general form of some of the specific irrational beliefs to which your client may adhere. When you help your clients to dispute a specific form of an irrational belief, they will be able to deal more effectively with a specific negative activating event. Thus, showing a client that it is not an utter necessity to have her husband's approval may help her to take criticism from that individual without making herself unduly upset. When you assist your clients in disputing a *core* irrational belief, you convey general principles that may help them to deal more effectively with a wide variety of problematic A's. Teaching your clients that the approval of others, regardless of who they are, *never* has to be a condition for self-acceptance can help them to cope more effectively with criticism that they might receive from a variety of people (for example, a boss, a particular family member, casual acquaintances). Clients who deal with their core irrational beliefs will be better able to generalize their application of REBC principles across persons and situations.

Guidelines for dealing with core irrational beliefs

Keep the following points in mind as you attempt to help your clients to identify, challenge and replace their core irrational beliefs.

Look for common themes

As you work with your clients in counselling, look for common themes among the irrational beliefs that underpin their problems. A given client, for example, may present the following array of problems: hurt and depression in response to criticism from her husband; anxiety about approaching her boss for a rise in pay; non-assertive, submissive behaviour in her dealings with friends. As you work with this client on these problems, begin forming hypotheses concerning core irrational beliefs that may be implicated in all of them. In the present example, you may hypothesize that your client has a core approval-related must that underpins her emotional and behavioural difficulties.

Encourage clients to identify their own core irrational beliefs

Once you have formed a hypothesis as to a given client's core irrational beliefs, suggest to her that there may be a common cognitive theme running through the problems the two of you have targeted for change. Then, ask her if she can identify this theme herself. Prompting your client to do this sort of thinking on her own can help to prepare her for identifying core irrational beliefs on an independent basis after formal counselling has ended.

Encourage clients to engage in self-observation

After your client sees that a core irrational belief underpins a number of the problems she has been working on, encourage her within sessions to see if she can identify any other problems (perhaps as yet undiscussed by the two of you) that may be attributable to this belief. You can also suggest that she engage in self-observation between sessions to sharpen her awareness of how this belief may impact on other areas of her functioning. Identification of additional problems stemming from your client's core irrational belief can lead to formulation of additional home-work assignments for combating this belief. As an example, an approval needy client may conduct self-observation and become aware that she tends to be non-assertive with shop assistants. She might then take on the homework assignment of acting more assertively with such individuals as an additional way of challenging her core irrational belief. Note that with some clients it may be wise to wait until they have made some progress with their original presenting problems before prompting identification of other, related problem areas. Otherwise, they may experience confusion and feel overwhelmed at having so many things to work on at once.

Help clients to design a core rational philosophy

In working with your client on specific problem areas, you will help assist her in developing specific rational philosophies that are useful in coping with particular problematic A's. As you move on to identifying and challenging her core irrational beliefs, help her also to develop a core rational philosophy which will be useful for facing a wide variety of potential problematic A's. Encourage your client to look for opportunities to apply this new core rational philosophy.

Additional issues concerning core irrational beliefs

1   Do not assume that all of your client's problems stem from the same core irrational belief. Typically, clients will harbour more than one such belief. Also note that more than one core irrational belief may be implicated in the same problem (for example, procrastination stemming from core musts for approval *and* for comfort).

2   Be aware that some clients will not want to work on their core irrational beliefs, in so far as this involves self-observation and identification of additional problem areas. They may have entered counselling with the goal of working on a few, relatively circumscribed problem areas, and lack the desire to expand the focus of counselling to other areas of their functioning. It may be prudent to honour your client's preferences in this regard, as doing otherwise could threaten the therapeutic alliance.

3   Avoid the error of dealing only with the core, general form of your client's specific irrational beliefs. If you do not pay enough attention to dealing with your client's *specific* irrational beliefs, she may make limited progress in being better able to cope with her *specific* negative A's.

Key point

When you identify and deal with clients' core irrational beliefs, you increase the likelihood that they will be able to generalize their application of REBC principles across a variety of negative A's. Encourage your clients to be active participants in the process of identifying core irrational beliefs and the diverse ways in which these beliefs adversely affect their functioning. However, do not neglect to work on specific forms of clients' core irrational beliefs, and do not assume that the same core irrational belief underpins all of each client's problems.

14   Go for philosophic change, but be prepared to compromise

In point 2, we argued that it was important for you to ensure that your clients have reasonable goals for counselling. As Bordin (1979) noted, counsellors have goals for their clients as well and one hallmark of effective counselling is that you and your client agree on the goals. Maluccio (1979) showed that mental health workers frequently have more ambitious goals for client outcome than clients do themselves. This is certainly an issue that you need to think carefully about and in this point we will consider the relevant factors concerning the differing ambitions that you and your clients may have concerning what type of change is being sought.

Different types of change

REBC theory argues that there are different types of change and in this section we will briefly explain what these are.

Philosophic change

When your client achieves philosophic change, he succeeds in changing his beliefs from irrational to rational. Your client can achieve philosophic change on specific issues or in more general areas of his life. For example, he can come to believe that he does not need the approval of his boss (specific) or that he does not need the approval of people in general (general).

Inferential change

When your client achieves inferential change, he succeeds in modifying his distorted inferences about actual events, but would still think irrationally if these distorted inferences were not changed. For example, let us suppose that a client infers that if he says something stupid in a group setting then members of that group will think he is weird. He further believes that if this happened it would be terrible. If the client only achieves inferential change (that is, without the corresponding philosophic change) on this issue, he will come to see that his inference is distorted and that it is more likely that the people in the group either will not notice his remark or will be sympathetic. However, he will still have the underlying belief that it would be terrible if people in the group think he is weird and will be vulnerable to anxiety as long as he holds this irrational belief. As long as he continues to hold this belief, he is likely to reinvent distorted negative inferences about the same situation later on or create similar distorted inferences about other relevant situations.

REBC theory holds that for clients to achieve stable inferential change they first need to achieve a fair measure of philosophic change.

Changing actual negative A's

Clients may improve because they no longer face actual negative A's. This change in A may occur for the following reasons.

The negative event may cease to exist   In this situation the client no longer faces the negative A for two reasons. First, the client may leave the situation. For example, a man who is angry at his boss's sarcasm decides to leave his job. Once he leaves his job he is no longer angry because the negative A ceases to exist.

Secondly, the client does nothing to bring about a change in A which changes in the natural course of events. For example, the man who is angry at his boss's sarcasm stops being angry when his boss leaves the company. In this situation, the client's feelings change because the negative A that he has faced is no longer present.

Situations where the client improves because A no longer exists and the client has done nothing to bring about a change in that A contain very little learning for the client at any level. Indeed, it might even encourage the client to believe that he is powerless to change negative events and must thus either avoid them or wait for them to change naturally.

The client is able to effect change in the event so that it is no longer negative   In this situation, the client no longer faces A because he has managed successfully to change it. Thus, in the above example, the man is able to influence his boss to change his behaviour by the judicious use of assertive skills, with the result that A no longer exists; his boss now acts nicely to him rather than sarcastically as before. This situation is preferable to the one discussed above because at least in this type of 'A change' the client is actively doing something to improve his situation and successfully so, whereas in the other situation the client is not even trying to change the situation directly. However, in this situation the person is still vulnerable to making himself angry if his boss does not respond to his assertive endeavours because he has not effected a philosophic change in his anger-creating irrational beliefs.

The client distracts himself from the negative event   In this situation, the client cannot avoid the situation, but is able to distract himself from it either behaviourally or cognitively. Thus, in our example, the client may behaviourally throw himself into work or cognitively think of his impending summer holidays to avoid focusing on his boss's sarcasm.

Behavioural change

In behavioural change, the person effects a change in his behaviour without making any corresponding philosophic change. This may be helpful in situations where the client lacks certain key skills and improves by learning such skills as study skills, social skills and sexual skills. Effecting such a change often (but not always) leads the person to (a) experience more positive events in his life and (b) make more favourable inferences about his competence in the relevant area. However, the essence of the change is behavioural and any irrational beliefs the person has are left intact.

When to compromise

There are too many possible permutations to consider what kind of change to settle for when it is not possible to help your client to effect a philosophic change in his thinking. Thus, we will focus here on the important question of *when* to compromise.

In working to encourage your client to achieve a philosophic change, it is important that you persist with this strategy for a lengthy period of time. You will know that there are four irrational belief processes: musts, awfulizing, low frustration tolerance and self-/other-downing. When disputing your client's irrational beliefs, we suggest that you begin with one target irrational belief (a must, for example) and persist in challenging this until either you have helped him to change this belief or it seems unlikely that you will help him to change it. Only make this conclusion if you have tried all available strategies and they have failed. If you reach this conclusion, then switch to challenging another irrational belief (such as, awfulizing) and persist with this strategy until again you have helped him to change this belief or until you have exhausted all available techniques without success.

If you have reached the inescapable conclusion that you cannot help your client to make a philosophic change on any of the possible variants of an irrational belief after following the guidelines outlined in the previous paragraph, switch to helping your client to make an inferential change, a behavioural change or a change in A.

Once you have helped your client to effect a non-philosophic change, then it is worth returning to a philosophic focus, since it sometimes happens that clients are more susceptible to making a philosophic change once they have achieved another kind of change.

Key point

Persist with helping your clients to effect a philosophic change in their beliefs until it is clear that this strategy will not bear fruit. If the latter is the case, switch to helping them to effect another kind of change (inferential, behavioural, changing A). Realize that it is irrational to stick rigidly with a philosophic strategy.

---

15 Be creative in your use of REBC

Whilst learning the fundamentals of REBC practice, you will have been encouraged to follow precise practical guidelines. Since REBC is a structured approach to counselling it does offer you a map to follow. For example, it outlines a 13-step guide to the counselling sequence in which you are urged to deal with your client's individual target problems (Dryden, 1990). In addition, when you come to dispute your client's irrational beliefs you are shown that there are three major arguments (namely, logical, empirical and pragmatic) and are generally given examples of questions to employ when using each argument (Dryden, 1995b).

In general, trainees appreciate the amount of help they are given to practise REBC despite the fact that they soon come to see that it is harder to practise it well than they first thought. You will have learned that if you persist with using the guidelines that you have been given, then you will gradually become more competent and thereby more confident as an REBC practitioner.

However, while undergoing this learning process you will have learned something else. You will have discovered that different clients have different responses to different aspects of the REBC assessment and treatment process. Indeed, as you gain more experience with a wider range of clientele you will appreciate the importance of developing personalized interventions with your clients. It is here that you need to develop creativity in your practice of REBC. How can you do this?

The REBC literature

While it is true that other people's writings on REBC cannot make you creative, they can certainly give you ideas about the kind of strategies and techniques that others have considered creative. The point of consulting the REBC literature is not to copy other people's ideas, although you will want to add such techniques to your therapeutic armamentarium; no, the purpose is to allow others' ideas to stimulate the development of your own. To this end, we suggest that you consult the following three texts which are a rich source of clinical ideas.

1   *Howard Young – Rational Therapist: Seminal Papers on Rational-Emotive Therapy* (edited by Windy Dryden). Loughton, Essex: Gale Centre Publications, 1989.

This book presents the late Howard Young's most important papers on REBC. Howard worked with a predominantly working class population in West Virginia, USA. His papers are full of innovative techniques and show the inner workings of a very creative therapist.

2   *The RET Resource Book for Practitioners* (edited by Michael Bernard and Janet Wolfe). New York: Institute for Rational-Emotive Therapy, 1993.

This book presents a veritable treasure trove of clinical techniques and procedures from many of the world's leading REBC counsellors.

3   *Doing RET: Albert Ellis in Action* (by Joseph Yankura and Windy Dryden). New York: Springer, 1990.

In this book, we present a comprehensive analysis of the therapeutic practice of Albert Ellis, the founder of REBC. As the subtitle of the book indicates, we show Albert Ellis in action through the extensive use of verbatim extracts between Ellis and his clients.

Video tapes and audio tapes

For many years, counselling trainees' first introduction to REBC has been the video of Albert Ellis counselling Gloria (who was also counselled by Fritz Perls and Carl Rogers in the early 1960s). The Ellis interview was about 20 minutes long and was not even a good demonstration of REBC as it was then. Ellis still holds that he tried to cram too much into this interview with the result that Gloria is not given much time to process the ground that she covers with Ellis.

Luckily the Institute for RET in New York has made available other more recent demonstrations of REBC that are truer representations of this counselling approach. In particular, we recommend the two videos showing Richard Wessler in action in the early 1980s and the very recent (1993) four video series showing Ray DiGiuseppe, Dom DiMattia, Albert Ellis and Janet Wolfe at work with four different clients. We recommend that you study these videos in detail and repeat your viewing several times, since they are rich in strategy and technique.

In addition, the Institute has a professional library of audio tapes of actual therapy sessions which are well worth studying, although the sound quality of many of the tapes leaves much to be desired. However, overcoming your LFT about this will be worth it. I (W.D.) am sure that repeated study of these tapes helped to stimulate my own creativity as an REBC counsellor.*

Give yourself permission to cultivate creative associations

I (W.D.) found that as my confidence as an REBC counsellor grew I was able to give myself permission to be creative. I stopped thinking about how Albert Ellis or Richard Wessler would respond and started thinking about how I, Windy Dryden, could respond. It sounds strange looking back at this time, but I remember it as a growth point in my therapeutic development. Having given myself permission to think for myself and not like my mentors I started to make associations which proved to be creative. In this period, I developed the principle of 'Vivid REBC' where the counsellor can increase her therapeutic potency by using memorable or vivid techniques (see Dryden, 1986, for an overview). I find that I can do this quite easily now, but remember that it was not always so easy.

I notice that much of my creativity is tinged with humour which reflects my personality. For example, in a recent group, I found myself disputing the irrational demand of a client named Pru by asking: 'Where is the law of the PRUniverse that you must. . .?' When I say that I found myself saying this, I mean just that; there was little premeditative thought involved. However, let me stress that this ability has been hard won and many a client has groaned at my less successful puns.

Having said this, we do not want you to be creative in Windy Dryden's or anybody else's image. If humour is not your thing, do not force it. Develop your creativity in your own way.

---

* To order these video tapes and audio tapes, contact the Institute for RET, 45 East 65th St, New York, NY 10021, USA.

Write your own rational humorous songs

Albert Ellis has noted that one way of viewing emotional disturbance is to see it as taking things *too* seriously. Consequently, he has penned numerous rational humorous songs which encourage clients to take a light-hearted (but not flippant) perspective on the events of their lives about which they disturb themselves (see Ellis, 1977).

I (W.D.) have found that another way of stimulating my creativity is to write such songs. It seems to me that it is the attempt to make the stanzas rhyme that is particularly useful in stimulating my creative thought. We invite you to write your own rational humorous songs to see what we mean. We close this section with Windy's latest effort which demonstrates the self-defeating aspects of guilt.

It Has To Be Me (to the tune of 'It Had To Be You')

It has to be me
It has to be me
Guilt is my game
I am to blame
It has to be me.

If something goes wrong
Who can it be?
It's the same old song
It's got to be me
It has to be me
Who else could it be?
It has to be me.

It has to be me
It has to be me
Guilt is my game
I am to blame
It has to be me.

If someone is hurt
The story's the same
You can bet your shirt
That I am to blame
It has to be me
Conceited old me
It has to be me.

> **Key point**
>
> Developing basic competence as an REBC counsellor frequently involves following precise practical guidelines. Once you have achieved this basic competence, you are ready to give yourself permission to be creative as an REBC counsellor. Using the REBC literature, studying REBC video tapes and audio tapes and composing your own rational humorous songs are three ways in which you can cultivate your own creative REBC associations.

16 Help your clients to develop an alternative rational philosophy

Kuhn (1970) has pointed out that scientists are more likely to reject an old theory when a new and better one becomes available. Picking up on this point, DiGiuseppe (1991) has advocated that counsellors explicitly help their clients to develop an alternative rational philosophy with which to replace their irrational beliefs. When clients have an alternative rational philosophy at their disposal, they are less likely to revert back to their irrational beliefs (and thus experience disturbance) when faced with a negative A.

It would be an error to assume that your clients will formulate, on their own, an alternative rational philosophy after you have thoroughly disputed their irrational beliefs. Thus, it makes good clinical sense for you to take steps to ensure your clients understand and are able to access a complex of rational beliefs that will be more helpful to them when they are confronted by negative A's.

Guidelines for developing an alternative rational philosophy

Keep the following points in mind as you work with clients to help them develop alternative rational philosophies with which to replace their irrational beliefs.

Encourage clients to think for themselves

It is more productive for your clients to be active than passive participants in the process of developing a rational philosophy with which to replace their self-defeating irrational beliefs. When your clients take an active role, they will probably have better recall of your teaching points and will have gained some experience that will help them to apply REBC on an independent basis. Your skilful use of questions represents a vehicle for engaging your clients as active participants.

After conducting pragmatic disputing of a particular irrational belief, for example, you could ask the following:

> If believing that it is absolutely *awful* to be rejected leads you into anxious avoidance, what could you believe instead that would be more helpful to you?

When your client responds to questions like this, check to be sure that his answer actually does constitute a component of a rational philosophy with respect to the issue at hand. If it does not, suggest a more rational alternative and explain why this is likely to be more helpful.

Show your client why the new philosophy is rational

Just as irrational beliefs tend to be illogical, inconsistent with reality and self-defeating, rational beliefs will tend to be logical, consistent with reality and self-enhancing. It is important for your client to see these points about the new rational philosophy you are helping him to develop, as this will probably help to strengthen his conviction in it. In order to do this, you can subject your client's new rational philosophy to the same sorts of disputes you used to challenge his irrational beliefs. Thus, for example, you could say to your client:

> We've agreed that the belief, 'I'm a failure if I fail my exam' is really illogical and will be unhelpful to you. The alternative belief we've come up with is 'If I fail, I'm never a Failure with a capital F. I'm just a fallible human being who sometimes does well and sometimes makes mistakes.' Can you explain to me why this alternative belief is more logical, more consistent with reality and potentially more helpful?

Assess and deal with client objections to the new, rational philosophy

Occasionally, clients will have reservations about the alternative rational philosophy you have helped them to construct. As an example, some bright, achievement-oriented clients will object to the notion of replacing their absolutistic musts with wants and preferences. These individuals hold the view that their musts represent an important source of achievement motivation for them. They believe that without certain musts in operation (for example, 'I *must* do an excellent job with this report for the board of directors!') they will become lazy and their performance will suffer. Such clients can be shown that their musts may often actually interfere with optimal performance (by contributing to performance-impairing negative emotions such as anxiety), and that their strong desires and wants can represent a sufficient source of motivation for getting a job done well.

Not all clients will be direct in expressing their objections to an alternative rational philosophy. As such, it is good practice for you to take steps to determine whether a client harbours un-expressed reservations about the new philosophy you have helped him to develop. This can be accomplished with a simple inquiry such as the following.

> We've just been discussing how the belief – 'It's inconvenient to get rejected, but hardly the end of the world' – stands as a rational alternative to the belief that it's absolutely *awful* to be rejected. Thinking about it now, do you have any objections to the idea that rejection is merely inconvenient and never *awful*?

If your client expresses some objections, take the time to try to deal with these before proceeding with any other counselling tasks.

Review and summarize the new rational philosophy

After you have worked with your client to identify the components of a more helpful rational philosophy of relevance to his problems, it is useful to review and summarize this with him. You may suggest that he writes it down (or tape records it) and reviews it frequently, so that he is able to access it more readily when confronted with problematic A's.

Use the rational philosophy to design helpful homework
assignments

After developing a rational philosophy with your client, you can use it as a vehicle for identifying useful homework assignments. In order to do so, ask your client a question such as the following:

> If you *really* believed that rejection is only inconvenient and never awful, how would you then tend to act at the party you've been invited to this weekend?

In this example, the client may respond that he would be more likely to start conversations with attractive strangers. This can then be suggested as a behavioural homework assignment to help him internalize his new rational beliefs.

Key point

As you work at disputing your clients' irrational beliefs, make sure that you take specific steps to help them develop a new, alternative rational philosophy. Do not assume that they will do this on their own without your assistance. Clients who are able to access an alternative rational philosophy when they are confronted with a negative A will probably be less likely to fall back to their upset-provoking irrational beliefs.

---

17   Check your clients' progress on a regular basis

As you proceed through counselling with a given client, you will probably have a sense as to how much progress this individual is making on the problems the two of you have targeted for change. This 'sense' will be derived from a number of factors, including each client's response to your disputing interventions and their success in carrying out homework assignments. It is, however, a good idea to step back periodically from your work on target problems and conduct – with your clients' agreement and co-operation – formal progress reviews. Such reviews allow you to:

1   Determine whether your clients are indeed making progress on their target problems.
2   See whether your perceptions as to your clients' progress agree with their own perceptions in this regard.
3   Identify and deal with obstacles that may be blocking your clients' progress on particular problems.

We recommend that you explain to your clients early on in treatment the benefits of regular progress reviews. Try to reach some general agreement as to the frequency with which the two of you will conduct such reviews. At the very least, near the start of counselling, attempt to establish at what point in the future the two of you will conduct your first progress review. You can do this by making the following sort of statement:

> I'd suggest that we have our first progress review during our fifth session. This will give us a chance to check on your initial response to your counselling and to deal with any questions or concerns that you may have at that point. How does that sound to you?

In the sections that follow we provide some additional guidelines for conducting formal progress reviews.

Use your client's problem list as a basis for conducting a progress review

In point 2 we introduced the idea of encouraging your client to construct a problem list at the start of counselling. Such a list helps you to make sure that your client has reasonable goals for her REBC, and can assist in structuring the entire course of counselling. You can also use your client's problem list when the two of you conduct your formal progress review. Run down the problem areas contained on your client's list one by one, and ask her how she views her progress on each item.

Maintain your focus during a progress review

During the course of a progress review, some clients will go off on tangents which make it difficult to ascertain progress on particular target problems. A given client may, for example, start to describe the details of a new problem she has encountered before finishing discussion of progress on a problem previously targeted for change. When this occurs, bring the client back tactfully to the issue at hand. You can suggest to her that the two of you can give further attention to her new problem after completing your review.

Some clients will attempt to change the topic during a progress review because they are ashamed of their lack of progress on a given problem. Be alert to this possibility, such that you can help your client to challenge the irrational belief that underpins her feeling of shame.

Be alert to your client's criteria for 'measuring' change

As you ask your client how she views her progress on each of her target problems, attempt to elicit from her the factors upon which she bases her perceptions. This can be done with the following sort of question: 'Can you describe to me specifically what tells you you've made progress on this problem?' Alternatively, you can ask your client to describe the most recent, significant instance in which she was aware of having progressed in a given problem area (for example, 'Tell me about a recent time when you were really aware of being more assertive with your in-laws').

It is important for you to determine early on the means by which your client 'measures' meaningful change for herself. In some instances, it may be advisable for you to suggest alternative indicants of progress to your client when she uses indicants that are imprecise or unreasonable. A socially phobic client new to REBC may, for example, view progress as meaning she will *never* again experience anxiety in social situations. With such a broad and unrealistic criterion for progress in mind, this client may ultimately become disillusioned with the counselling process and drop out of treatment. In order to prevent this, it would be helpful to teach her to instead view her progress in terms of the intensity, duration and frequency with which she experiences anxiety in social situations.

Check the basis of change

As per REBC theory, clients will make progress in counselling and become less vulnerable to emotional disturbance as they work at surrendering and replacing their upset-producing irrational beliefs. It is not uncommon, however, for clients to find less constructive, potentially self-defeating strategies for dealing with their emotional problems. As mentioned in point 14, these strategies include:

1   changing inferences about a negative A;
2   attempts to change, avoid or distract oneself from fully experiencing a negative A;
3   making behavioural changes without changing operative irrational beliefs.

While all of these strategies may lead clients to report seemingly beneficial changes in their negative C's, they leave clients vulnerable to future emotional disturbance. As such, when your client reports positive changes in C during a progress review, check to be sure what underlies these changes. If your inquiry reveals that your client is employing one or several of the strategies listed above, and it is your impression that she is capable of making philosophic change, encourage her to refocus her efforts on challenging and replacing her irrational beliefs. Make sure your client understands the potential benefits of making such efforts.

Check for new problems

During a progress review, it is a good idea to see if your client has any new, additional problems that she would like to work on. If she does, attempt to define reasonable goals with respect to these new problems and come to some agreement as to when you will work on them. Does your client want to turn attention to the new problems right away? Or, would she prefer to postpone work on the new problems and maintain a focus on the problems the two of you already have been working on?

Negotiate updated goals

New or updated goals can be one important product of a formal progress review. Negotiate with your client to determine what step, or goal, she would next like to reach with respect to a target problem that requires further work. Define this updated goal in realistic and specific terms, and help your client to get clear on what she needs to do to approach it.

Be aware of your client's feelings when conducting progress reviews

When giving feedback concerning your client's efforts during a progress review, be aware of her emotional reactions to this feedback. If your client perceives your feedback to be corrective in nature, she may engage in negative self-rating because she believes that she *should not* make mistakes in counselling. If you suspect that your client is engaging in this sort of self-downing in relation to your feedback, assess this and deal with it as you would with other emotional problems.

Key point

It is advisable periodically to conduct formal progress reviews with your clients. Such reviews allow you to assess whether clients are deriving optimal benefits from their REBC. When conducting a progress review, you can check the basis for changes in negative C's, identify new problems to work on and negotiate updated goals.

---

18 Watch out for and deal with your clients' irrational beliefs about counselling

You will find that clients sometimes subscribe to irrational beliefs about aspects of their REBC counselling that may impede their progress and in some cases contribute to premature termination. In order to prevent these irrational beliefs from becoming a significant obstacle to client progress, it is important that you identify them and help your client to dispute them. In the sections that follow, we discuss some of the more common irrational beliefs that clients may bring to bear upon their counselling experience.

'Counselling should be easy; it's too hard to work at changing myself!'

This irrational belief contributes to low frustration tolerance and discomfort disturbance. Clients who subscribe to this belief may manifest frequent non-compliance with homework assignments, have sporadic attendance of sessions, and may appear to become annoyed at you when you attempt to get them to work (as when you use Socratic disputing) within counselling sessions. If you suspect that your client harbours this belief and is deriving limited benefits from counselling because of it, bring it to your client's attention and encourage her to work with you on dealing with it. You can use your client's non-compliance with a homework assignment as a vehicle for assessing whether this belief is in operation. For example, you might ask your client: 'What do you think you might have been telling yourself about the discomfort involved in doing this homework exercise?'

'I need my counsellor's help and support; I'm too weak to help myself!'

When your client strongly subscribes to this irrational belief, she will be likely to form a dependent relationship with you. If this belief goes unidentified and unaddressed, it will interfere with your client's progress in learning to become an independent emotional problem-solver. It may also cause counselling to be needlessly prolonged. When this irrational belief is operative for your client, she may be prone to engage in the following sorts of behaviours.

1   Evincing helplessness at various points during sessions (for example, when you ask her to challenge a particular irrational belief or to try to design a homework assignment relevant to a particular problem).
2   Phoning you between sessions to get help and support with relatively minor problems that may arise during the week.
3   Frequently and anxiously checking with you as to whether you have any plans to move away or become ill in the near future, such that you would become unavailable to her.
4   Consistently failing to do homework assignments that seem well within her capacity to enact.

When it appears to you that your client holds a dependency-producing belief, attempt to explore this possibility with your client so that she can, if appropriate, work at challenging and replacing it. Such exploration can be initiated by making the following sort of statement to your client:

> There's something I'd like to check out with you that has relevance to how your counselling proceeds. In order to do so, I'd like to describe an imaginary scenario to you. Here it is: Imagine that at your next session, I suddenly announce to you that within the next month I will be moving far away. How would you feel?

Here, your client has been provided with an imaginary negative A and is being asked to describe the emotional C she would experience in connection with it. If she responds to this query by indicating that she would experience an unhealthy negative C, you can then work with her to identify the irrational beliefs underpinning this C. Her dependency-producing belief may thus be brought to light, and the negative consequences of holding this belief discussed. Encourage your client to target this belief for change.

'I must not risk my counsellor's disapproval; it would be awful if my counsellor thought poorly of me!'

This belief can impede clients from being active participants within their own counselling, in so far as it contributes to non-assertive behaviour and may lead your client to profess automatic agreement with everything you suggest during sessions. It may also lead clients to be less than honest with you when you check on their homework compliance or their understanding of your teaching points. For example, a given client – in order to avoid 'offending' you – may report that she fully completed her homework assignment when this really was not the case. Be alert to signs that your client's behaviour within counselling appears to be motivated by a fear of your disapproval. If you accumulate enough behavioural evidence to suggest that this is the case, take the following steps.

1   Tactfully communicate your suspicions about this issue to your client.
2   Tell her it is not uncommon for clients to believe they *must* have their counsellor's approval.

3 Show her how her irrational belief may interfere with her progress.
4 Encourage her to work with you on challenging and replacing this belief.

Also, explain to your client that as an REBC counsellor your stance is not to judge your clients globally on the basis of their actions (as REBC counsellors strive to offer their clients unconditional acceptance).

'I should always do my homework; the fact that I don't proves that I'm no good!'

Some clients, after they understand the REBC model of change, will absolutistically demand of themselves that they must always comply with homework assignments. When for some reason they fail to do their homework, they then apply some sort of global negative rating to themselves (for example, 'I'm . . . a failure/lazy/a weak person/a hopeless case' etc.).

When clients base a global rating of themselves upon their performance with homework assignments, they run the risk of making their counselling into an aversive, anxiety-laden experience for themselves. Also, they may tend to do their homework assignments for the 'wrong' reason (that is, in order to avoid a negative global rating of themselves). If your client appears overly dejected or otherwise upset when she reports to you that she neglected to do her homework for a given week, consider that she may be placing absolutistic performance demands upon herself. If you determine that this is the case, show her that: (a) no one is 100 per cent successful with homework assignments in counselling, and (b) it is counterproductive, illogical and empirically incorrect for her to rate herself negatively when she fails to do them. Also, be sure to explore the reasons for homework non-compliance with your client. There may be obstacles to homework enactment that need to be dealt with (see points 26 and 27).

'Now that I understand rational thinking and have made some progress, I must always think rationally and never backslide!'

Clients who subscribe to this irrational belief will be prone to engage in negative self-rating when they perceive that they have upset themselves about an A which they had previously made some progress in dealing with. If your client reports disturbing herself about something between sessions and appears depressed or angry at herself as she relates this, consider that she may harbour this belief. Assess whether your hypothesis in this regard is correct, and then, first, point out to her that it is not uncommon for clients to apply *musts* to their use of REBC, secondly explain that backsliding is to be expected as one works at changing one's beliefs, and thirdly engage her in working to dispute and replace her irrational belief. Also, you can suggest to your client that she obtain and read Ellis's (1984) pamphlet entitled, 'How to maintain and enhance your rational-emotive therapy gains'. This pamphlet contains a section for clients on how to deal with backsliding.

Key point

Clients may sometimes have irrational beliefs about counselling which can cause them to disturb themselves about various aspects of their counselling experiences. Be alert to this phenomenon, such that you can intervene and prevent these beliefs from becoming a significant obstacle to client progress.

---

19 Identify and deal with obstacles to change

Obstacles to change can pervade the entire counselling process. REBC counsellors attempt to be alert to these obstacles, such that they can be actively dealt with. Obstacles to change within counselling can be viewed as falling into four major categories.

1 Those that occur within the counselling relationship between counsellor and client.
2 Those that can be attributed to variables specific to the client.
3 Those that can be attributed to aspects of the client's external environment.
4 Those that can be attributed to variables specific to the counsellor.

Each of these categories will be briefly reviewed, and suggestions for dealing with them will be presented.

Obstacles to change within the counselling relationship

It occasionally happens that the match between counsellor and client is not an optimal one. When this occurs, it may be wise to make a judicious referral to a different REBC counsellor. In addition, some clients may have expectations and preferences for the way their counselling proceeds that you, as an REBC counsellor, may be unwilling to meet. If this is the case, referral to another sort of counsellor may be appropriate.

It is also the case that counsellors may sometimes adopt a therapeutic style which is not beneficial for certain clients. A counsellor with an overly warm style, for instance, may inadvertently reinforce a given client's approval-related musts. Another counsellor with a very active-directive style may encourage passivity in a client who tends to be non-assertive and submissive. It is important for you to be aware of the style of interaction you bring to the counselling process, and to monitor how this style is impacting on your clients. If it appears to you that a given style is having a negative impact on the change process for one of your clients, try experimenting with an alternative style and monitor the client's response to it.

Obstacles to change specific to the client

As noted in point 18, clients will sometimes subscribe to irrational beliefs which interfere with their progress in counselling. You can bring such beliefs to your client's attention, show him how they impede his counselling progress, and attempt to engage him in the process of surrendering them.

Picking up on the issue of the discomfort involved in change, Maultsby (1984) has noted that clients sometimes experience a feeling of 'strangeness' as they attempt to surrender their irrational beliefs and adopt rational ones. Encourage your client to accept this feeling as a natural part of the change process, and help him to dispute any beliefs he has that he *must* feel natural and comfortable all of the time.

Some achievement-oriented clients may be reluctant to give up their musts because they believe them to be an important source of achievement motivation. They believe that unless they put absolutistic demands for success upon themselves, they will fail to accomplish their important goals in life. Convey to such clients that their strong desires and preferences are a sufficient source of motivation, and help them to see the ways in which their irrational beliefs have resulted in needless upsets and obstacles to attainment of valued goals.

Other clients may hesitate to become engaged in counselling because they have misconceptions about how REBC will affect them. Dryden and Gordon (1990), for instance, have pointed out that some individuals fear that REBC will make them into unfeeling robots. This, of course, is not a goal of REBC, which holds that certain types of negative emotions (such as disappointment, regret and annoyance) are actually healthy and helpful. When you become aware that clients harbour misconceptions about REBC, attempt to correct these as effectively as possible.

Obstacles to change within the client's environment

The interpersonal and social environments within which your clients live can sometimes interfere with their progress in counselling (Golden, 1983). Two categories of environmental obstacles are the following.

Sabotage from significant others

Significant others within your client's interpersonal environment may sometimes wilfully or unknowingly sabotage her efforts to overcome her emotional/behavioural problems. As an example of wilful sabotage, your client's spouse may threaten to walk out on her if she continues to become more assertive within their relationship. Inadvertent sabotage by significant others can occur when they unknowingly act in ways that reinforce your client's problems. A family member, for instance, may reinforce a given client's agoraphobic avoidance by offering to run errands that the client could conceivably take care of personally. When family members or friends knowingly or unknowingly interfere with the changes your client would like to make through counselling, you can consider inviting them to counselling sessions in order to try to enlist their support. When such individuals cannot legitimately be invited to sessions, your client can specifically be taught how to deal with them (Ellis's 1975 book, *How to Live with a Neurotic*, can be a helpful resource for achieving this end). If the above strategies prove impractical or ineffective, you may discuss with your client the possible wisdom of distancing himself or removing himself from interpersonal situations that inhibit his growth.

Secondary gains

Clients sometimes experience secondary gains for maintaining their emotional/behavioural problems. Thus, a dependent, non-assertive female client may gain the 'advantage' of being protected within the sheltering relationship she has with her domineering husband, as long as she continues to behave in a submissive manner toward him. It is also noted that some individuals may receive financial assistance from government agencies because they have certain sorts of disabilities. As improved functioning could result in the termination of this financial assistance, they may experience ambivalence about using counselling to overcome their problems. When issues related to secondary gains impact on your clients' progress in counselling, encourage them to examine the long-term benefits they may accrue if they give up the short-term benefits of their secondary gains.

Obstacles to change specific to the counsellor

The various points discussed within this book will help you to avoid or deal effectively with many of the errors that counsellors commonly make as they conduct REBC with their clients. Recognize that client 'resistance' is frequently a result of counsellor error, and that it is advisable for you constantly to monitor the effects that your actions and interventions have upon your clients. Regardless of theoretical orientation, counsellors are often too willing to blame poor counselling outcomes upon factors specific to the client (Lazarus and Fay, 1982).

In *A Practitioner's Guide to Rational-Emotive Therapy* (2nd edition), Walen, DiGiuseppe and Dryden (1992) present an RET supervision form that you may find useful in conducting self-supervision of your counselling sessions. You can check your activities within a session against the items contained on this form. In addition to conducting self-supervision, however, it is important for you to seek regular supervision from another experienced REBC counsellor. This issue receives further discussion in point 29.

Counsellors' irrational beliefs about the work that they do with their clients can be another source of obstacles within the counselling process. This issue is discussed in point 28.

Key point

Throughout the counselling process, watch for and deal with obstacles to change stemming from:

1 problems in the counselling relationship;
2 client variables;
3 variables related to the client's environment;
4 counsellor variables.

As a general guideline, it is desirable to often ask yourself the following questions: 'Is my client benefiting from his or her REBC? If not, why?'

For further details on dealing with obstacles to change within REBC, we refer you to Dryden and Yankura (1993), Ellis (1985) and Golden (1983).

III

Helping Clients to Use
REBC between
Counselling Sessions

20 Encourage your clients to work independently at REBC throughout the counselling process

Most clients will derive benefits from REBC in proportion to the degree to which they work independently at their counselling. In addition, clients who make independent efforts during the course of counselling will probably be better able to act as their own therapists after counselling has ended. As such, you will want to find ways to encourage and promote independent effort on your clients' part. Some suggestions germane to this issue are provided below.

Emphasize the importance of homework assignments

Dryden (1990) has pointed out that 'the main burden of responsibility for promoting client change rests on your client carrying out homework assignments between sessions' (p. 78). This is because homework assignments present an opportunity for your clients to practise disputing their irrational beliefs and to internalize a new, rational philosophy. A good number of clients, however, will enter counselling with the notion that they are only supposed to 'work' at it during their sessions with you. As such, explain the role and importance of homework assignments to your client quite early-on in the counselling process. Also, ensure that homework assignments are used regularly throughout counselling, as this will serve to reinforce in your clients' minds the importance they carry (see also points 22 and 26).

Encourage your clients to become more active during sessions

During the beginning phase of REBC, you will probably want to be quite active-directive with most clients in order to help them quickly learn the essentials of the REBC change process. As counselling proceeds, however, it is a good idea to become somewhat less active-directive and to require your clients to do more of the work during sessions. Thus, after your clients have experienced some success in learning and applying REBC methods to some of their problems, encourage them to take the lead in working at resolving subsequent emotional problems that become a focus of treatment. You may accomplish this by using the following sorts of questions.

- How would you analyse that problem with the ABC model?
- What irrational belief do you think was in operation when you became upset about A?
- How could you dispute that irrational belief?
- What could you tell yourself to prevent an upset the next time you confront A?

Encourage clients to design their own homework assignments

Just as you would prompt your clients to take more of the responsibility for the work that occurs within sessions, you can also encourage them to take more responsibility for what happens *between* sessions. As counselling proceeds, try to engage clients in designing their own homework assignments. You can prompt them to do so by first recapping what the two of you have worked on during a given session, and then asking the client how she might continue this work on her own during the week. When prompting your client to design her own homework, however, refrain from using a general sort of question such as 'What would you like to do as homework this week?' Often clients who are still learning about the REBC change process will respond to such a question by describing a homework assignment that is either unrelated to the issue discussed during the current session and/or has little or nothing to do with the process of disputing and replacing irrational beliefs. It is preferable to use a more specific sort of prompting question, such as 'How could you work at practising the new rational philosophy we developed during this session?'

Extend the time between sessions

Initially, you may be meeting with your clients for sessions once each week. As they make progress in dealing with their problems, you may want to consider extending the time prior to your next meeting with them. This can give them additional time to practise being their own therapists through applying the methods they have learned in their REBC. If it appears to you that this course of action would be beneficial for a particular client, broach the issue as a collaborative decision that you and the client will make together. Allow an opportunity for your client to voice any doubts or fears she has about extending the time between sessions, and deal with these as appropriate.

Deal with clients' irrational beliefs about working independently

Some clients may cling to the belief that they *must* have the assistance of a person more knowledgeable or stronger than themselves if they are to overcome their emotional problems. This belief may cause them to become dependent upon their counsellors, and they may make themselves anxious when they are encouraged to work more independently. Be alert to client dependency, such that you can deal with the beliefs underpinning it when it arises.

Show appreciation of clients' efforts to work independently

When your clients attempt to function as their own therapists, reinforce their efforts. This can help to encourage them to extend these attempts as counselling proceeds. Too often, novice REBC counsellors neglect to comment favourably upon the efforts that their clients *do* make to complete their homework assignments. Be cautious, however, about the manner in which you reinforce client efforts. You do not want inadvertently to reinforce a client's approval-neediness or self-rating tendencies (for example, 'What a great person I am for working so hard in counselling!').

Key point

Encourage clients to work independently at REBC in order to facilitate their progress and prepare them to act as their own counsellors after counselling has ended. You can accomplish this by:

1 emphasizing why homework assignments are important;
2 encouraging your clients to become more active during counselling sessions;
3 encouraging your clients to design their own homework assignments;
4 extending the time between sessions;
5 dealing with your clients' irrational beliefs about working more independently;
6 reinforcing independent efforts that your clients make.

---

21 Encourage your clients to work at counselling in cognitive, behavioural and emotive modalities

REBC acknowledges the principle of psychological interactionism, which holds that cognition, behaviour and emotion all significantly overlap and influence each other (Dryden and Yankura, 1993). As such, REBC counsellors adopt a multimodal approach to counselling and encourage their clients to utilize cognitive, emotive and behavioural methods in the service of therapeutic change. When clients attack their beliefs through several modalities, they stand a better chance of surrendering their upset-producing irrational beliefs and internalizing a new, more helpful rational philosophy. Also, when clients employ a variety of methods to work at overcoming their emotional problems, they are more likely to remain interested and engaged in the counselling process (Dryden, 1990).

In order to teach your clients how to work at change through the cognitive, behavioural and emotive modalities, you will have to familiarize yourself with the armamentarium of techniques favoured by REBC counsellors. Since a complete review of these techniques is beyond the scope of the present section, we refer you to Dryden and Yankura (1993) and Walen, DiGuiseppe and Dryden (1992) for further reading. In the section below, however, we provide a case example of how a particular client was helped to take a multimodal approach to changing her irrational beliefs and overcoming her emotional/behavioural problems.

Case example: examination anxiety

Sue, a 23-year-old graduate student in psychology, was due to take a comprehensive examination that she needed to pass in order to proceed to the next level of her course of study. She sought counselling because she was experiencing anxiety in connection with her upcoming examination and was avoiding the task of studying. After conducting a thorough assessment of her problems, she and her counsellor agreed that she was probably subscribing to the following two irrational beliefs:

1 'I simply *must* pass my examination; if I don't my fellow students will think I'm a dolt, and that would be *awful!*'.
2 'Studying *should* be more interesting than it is; I *can't tolerate* an activity that's so monotonous.'

Sue's counsellor taught her to dispute these beliefs within sessions, and worked with her to develop a series of cognitive, behavioural and emotive homework assignments that she was to carry out across several weeks.

Cognitive methods

With respect to *cognitive* homework assignments, Sue was first of all encouraged to tape record and review her counselling sessions (see point 23). This allowed her to have additional exposure to some of the teaching points and disputing arguments her counsellor presented to her. She was also helped to develop a number of rational coping self-statements (Ellis, 1979b), which she was encouraged to write down on a 3 × 5 index card. These self-statements included the following:

Even though I very much *want* to pass my exam, I don't absolutely *have to*. I don't *have to* have what I want!

If I *do* fail and other students judge me negatively, I'm not going to like it, but I certainly can stand it! Besides, I wouldn't be the first person ever to take the exam a second time.

Studying *is* uncomfortable for me, but I certainly *can* tolerate that discomfort to reach a desired goal!

Sue's counsellor suggested that she review these rational coping self-statements on a daily basis, in order to assist in the process of internalizing an alternative rational philosophy that would help her to study and sit for her exam with a minimum of anxiety.

Behavioural methods

Sue also enacted several behavioural homework assignments. She was prompted to schedule herself for study sessions several times during the week, and instructed on how to challenge her irrational beliefs (using REBC homework forms, discussed under point 24) if she found herself acting in an avoidant fashion when these study times arrived. Also, her counsellor taught her how to use rewards and penalties with herself to increase the likelihood that she would stick with her self-assigned study schedule. Here, it is noted that REBC particularly favours teaching chronically resistant clients how to use penalties with themselves to facilitate their completion of homework assignments. Ellis (1985) has noted that while resistant clients will often not work to obtain a reward, they will frequently be motivated to complete certain tasks in order to avoid a penalty.

Emotive methods

With respect to emotive homework assignments, Sue was taught how to make use of rational-emotive imagery (REI) (Maultsby and Ellis, 1974). She was instructed to imagine a scene in which she discovered – after checking the posting of grades in the presence of fellow students – that she had failed her comprehensive examination. She was to use this image to help bring on a feeling of anxiety. After making herself initially feel anxious in relation to this imagined scenario, she was to work in her own mind at changing her feelings of anxiety to a feeling of mere concern about the possibility that other students might think poorly of her. She was encouraged to try to effect this change in her feelings by changing her irrational philosophy, as opposed to doing so by simply changing the nature of her anxiety-provoking image (for example, imagining that fellow students were supportive rather than critical with respect to her exam failure). Sue took on the assignment of practising REI each morning for 10 minutes before leaving home for her first class. As another emotive method for working at change, Sue was instructed in how to dispute irrational beliefs in a particularly vigorous and evocative fashion (Dryden, 1990).

As a result of working on these varied fronts, Sue was able to minimize her anxiety and increase the amount of time she spent studying. She passed her exam by a comfortable margin. Although the heading of this section contained the phrase 'examination anxiety', it is here noted that Sue's problems can be viewed as involving both ego anxiety and discomfort anxiety.

Key point

Since cognition, behaviour and emotion significantly overlap and influence each other, your clients will probably make better progress in counselling when they work on their problems in cognitive, behavioural and emotive modalities. As such, it is advisable for you to teach your clients how to work at changing their irrational beliefs in a variety of ways.

---

22 Negotiate homework assignments

In this point we will briefly outline 10 ways in which you can improve your ability to negotiate homework assignments with your clients. For a more detailed discussion of these and other suggestions consult Dryden (1995b). Before we present these illustrative suggestions, however, we will say a word about the importance of *negotiating* homework assignments.

Why negotiate?

Why is it important to *negotiate* homework assignments with your clients? Why not just tell them what to do between therapy sessions or accept uncritically their suggestions for their own homework assignments – which are the two other possible approaches to homework? Before answering these questions, let us outline what we mean by *negotiating* homework assignments.

The negotiating approach to homework assignments

When you initiate the process of negotiating a homework assignment with a client, you will already have a good idea what she can do between sessions to further her learning and/or therapeutic progress. So as a first step in negotiating the assignment, you let her know what your suggestion is. If she accepts your suggestion, fine; but, if she does not, encourage her to tell you what her own ideas are concerning what her assignment should preferably be. After she has told you her ideas, you will then attempt to come to a mutual agreement concerning the assignment. Most of the time this will involve you encouraging your client to see that she can do more than she thinks she can, although there will be times when you will strive to restrain your client from doing more than is good for her.

In short, the essence of negotiation involves:

1   a frank exchange of views concerning the nature of the assignment;
2   a discussion of these viewpoints when they are different;
3   the establishment of a mutual agreement concerning the nature of the assignment.

We argue that if you adopt this tripartite negotiating approach to homework assignments, then you will achieve two things. First, you will increase the likelihood that your client will do the assignment and, secondly, you will strengthen the therapeutic alliance between the client and yourself.

The unilateral approach to homework assignments

When you unilaterally tell your client what she will do for homework, you do not elicit her views, permit any discussion of your 'instruction', or allow for any degree of mutuality. While there are undoubtedly *some* clients who will respond to this 'I am the expert, you will do what I tell you' stance, our experience as REBC trainers and supervisors has led us to the conclusion that this approach engenders quite a lot of client 'resistance' (see points 19 and 27).

The 'laissez-faire' approach to homework assignments

In this approach to homework assignments you ask your client what she wants to take as a homework assignment and you accept uncritically whatever she says. The problem with this approach to homework assignments is twofold. First, it depends on your client having a deep understanding of REBC theory such that she can determine for herself a relevant homework assignment. This is, of course, unlikely until the latter stages of counselling. Secondly, your client is, in reality, likely to suggest easy to achieve assignments which are likely to reinforce her philosophy of low frustration tolerance.

Ten ways of improving your skills at negotiating homework assignments

Having presented the case for negotiating homework assignments, let us now introduce 10 ways in which you can improve your skills at negotiating homework assignments. Space does not permit a comprehensive discussion of all relevant tips, but they will stimulate your own thinking on the subject.

1   Use a term for homework assignments that is acceptable to your client.

Not all clients respond well to the term 'homework assignment'. Indeed, some will wince at the term because it has negative associations with school. Find an alternative term that denotes homework, but which is more acceptable to your client.

2   Ensure that the homework assignment is relevant to your client's goals.

While negotiating the homework assignment keep your client's goals very much in mind. If the task is related to her goals then she is more likely to derive benefit from carrying it out than if it is not.

3   Express the homework assignment clearly.

While negotiating a homework assignment with your client, it is important that you express yourself clearly. Otherwise your client will not be sure what she is agreeing to.

4   Ensure that your client understands the homework assignment.

This tip is allied to the one presented above. It is important that your client understands the homework assignment, if she is going to do it. Ask her to put into her own words what she is agreeing to do between sessions.

5   Help your client understand the relevance of the homework assignment to her goals.

This tip is related to the second one we gave. Your client is more likely to do the assignment if she can see clearly that carrying it out is likely to help her achieve her goals than if she lacks this insight. The best way of doing this is to encourage her to put the purpose of the assignment into her own words.

6   Ensure that the homework assignment follows logically from the work that you and your client did in the session.

Your client will become quite confused if you suggest that she take as a homework assignment something that has little relevance to what you have discussed in the bulk of the counselling session. Suggesting an assignment that flows logically from the work that you have done in the session gives counselling an understandable continuity that the majority of clients appreciate.

7   Ensure that the assignment is relevant to the stage you and your client have reached on her target problem.

Here you may err in two respects. First, you may suggest an assignment that is too advanced for the work you have done with your client on her target problem. In which case, sensing that you think that she can do more than is feasible, your client may agree to undertake a task that is beyond what she can reasonably be expected to do. In this case she may become disenchanted when she fails to do the assignment. Secondly, you may suggest an assignment that is too unambitious. In doing so, you may communicate that you believe that your client needs to go very slowly and/or that she is not capable of doing anything more challenging to help herself. Suggesting an assignment that is relevant to the stage of work that you and your client are doing on her target problem is a deft skill which you need to discuss with your REBC supervisor (see point 29).

8   Introduce the 'no lose' concept of homework assignments.

The 'no lose' concept of homework assignments states that if your client does the assignment and benefits from it, then that is good because the client is improving. Secondly, if the client does the assignment, but does not benefit from it, then that is useful because it provides information concerning why the assignment was unsuccessful. Finally, if your client does not do the assignment, then that is also of some use because you and your client learn more about her 'resistance' and can respond accordingly.

Explaining this concept to clients often helps to dispel their fear of failure with respect to doing homework assignments.

9   Ensure that your client has the necessary skills to do the assignment.

Asking your client to do an assignment for which she lacks the necessary skills can be quite demoralizing for her. If the assignment is an important one, first teach her the relevant skills. Otherwise, only ask her to do something that is within her present repertoire of skills.

10 Allow yourself sufficient time at the end of the session to negotiate the homework assignment properly.

Too often we have heard REBC trainees allot insufficient time at the end of the session to negotiate homework assignments properly. In giving themselves only a moment or two, they tend not to implement the tips that we have suggested above and end up by assigning the task unilaterally. It is best to give yourself about 10 minutes to negotiate a properly constructed homework assignment until you develop competence in homework negotiation. Then you may be able to do it in less time. No matter how skilled you are as an REBC counsellor, however, it is best not to rush this important therapeutic task.

Key point

Negotiating homework assignments with clients is a delicate skill which requires much practice. Learn the three components of homework negotiation and bear in mind the 10 tips that we have offered you here as you negotiate.

23 Suggest that your clients record and review counselling sessions

When your client is talking, he is often preoccupied with a number of issues. Thus, he may be concentrating on what he is saying and how he is saying it; he may be wrapped up in the distressed emotions he is currently experiencing as well as with the associations he may be making for himself while he is speaking.

When you are talking to your client, he may be focusing on what he has just said or has just thought of at the same time as listening to the content of what you are saying. When you are teaching your client something didactically, he may lose track of what you are saying because of the length of what you are saying, the delivery of what you are saying or because his mind is wandering for other reasons. Similarly when you are engaging your client in a Socratic dialogue, your client may be attempting to figure out what you want to hear as well as trying to make sense of the purpose of your questions.

In short, there is much scope in REBC for a number of factors to impede your client's learning. Since you hope that your client will understand the determinants of his psychological problems and will learn methods to overcome these problems, you need to find ways to minimize the development of these impediments and find ways around them once they exist. Suggesting that your client record his counselling sessions for later review is one way that you can compensate for the barriers to client learning that we have just briefly reviewed. Incidentally, if your client agrees to record his counselling sessions, he is also likely to allow you to record the sessions for supervisory purposes (see point 29).

When you suggest that your client record his counselling sessions, the rationale that you need to give will incorporate the arguments that we put forward above, that is, that there are many factors that combine to prevent your client from getting as much from the session as he could. You will stress that later he will be in a more objective frame of mind than he was in the session to understand the points that you made in the session and the full implications of what he was saying himself.

What should clients listen for?

You can give your client the following suggestions concerning what he should listen for when he reviews the tape of the session.

The client should simply listen to the tape

First, you can give your client a general suggestion that he should listen to the tape without offering any specific recommendations concerning what he should listen to. Here, you are quite content for your client to pick up on issues that he finds relevant for discussion in the following session. This is the least directive stance you can take here.

The client should listen specifically to the points made by the counsellor

Secondly, you can give your client a specific suggestion that he should listen attentively to what you as counsellor had to say in the session. In particular, you can direct your client's attention to those segments of the session where you taught him some aspect of REBC theory that was relevant to his problem and how he can overcome it. Suggest to your client that he write down his reactions to your teaching points, noting in particular any dis- agreements that he had with the material. Since it is possible to consider reviewing counselling sessions as a client homework assignment, you can legitimately put 'listening to the counselling session' on the session agenda when you check your client's homework (see point 26). In particular, it is important that you elicit your client's disagreements with REBC theory so that you can correct any misunderstandings that he may have about what you said. Unless you correct your client's misconceptions, they will remain intact and will interfere with your client's learning.

You may also instruct your client to listen to specific inter- ventions that you made which you consider to be particularly important. Again, suggest that your client bring his reactions to the next session for discussion.

The client should listen to himself

Thirdly, you can suggest that your client listen closely to what *he* said in the session. Your suggestion here can range from the broad to the specific. At the broadest level, you can suggest that your client listen generally to what he said in the counselling session and report back his impressions in the following session. At the most specific level you can ask your client to listen to a narrow piece of behaviour and reflect on its meaning.

When you ask your client to listen to some aspect of his own behaviour, examples may include listening, in particular, for the understanding he showed of the rational concepts that you were teaching him and listening to his tendency to avoid identifying his feelings. The purpose of these suggestions is to elicit the client's opinion on an issue that you may have identified but wish to test out. If after listening to the tape he agrees that his understanding of the rational concepts was not as good as he thought or that he does tend to avoid his feelings, you are in a position to remedy the situation. Without access to the raw data of the tape, your client may well resist your observations.

In addition, you may ask your client to listen to the tape with the specific intention of having him think about (a) the problems he may have that he is not discussing, (b) reactions to the counselling process or to you as counsellor that he is keeping to himself or (c) irrational beliefs he may hold that he has previously denied having.

When *not* to ask your client to review counselling sessions

There are a number of situations when it is not advisable to suggest to your client that he records and reviews his counselling sessions. These are as follows.

Client self-condemnation

A number of clients will condemn themselves when they listen to tapes of their counselling sessions. They may put themselves down for what they say or for how they sound to themselves. You may be able to use this issue therapeutically, encouraging your client to listen to the tape again, focus on the 'shameful' material and accept himself as a fallible human being as he does this. Your client may not be able to do this and consequently you may suggest that he stop recording sessions for a while and take notes during counselling sessions instead.

Client dependency on the tapes

Some clients become dependent on the tapes of their counselling sessions. Rather than thinking through their problems in an active way, these clients prefer to listen passively to their tapes. Indeed, clients who are dependent on their tapes often keep detailed records of what is on each tape so that they can replay relevant sections instead of engaging actively in emotional problem-solving. Instead of using tapes as a *prompt*, they use them as a *crutch*. It is important to wean such clients from using taped sessions in this dependent way and to teach them how to be active in the therapeutic change process. However, we would prefer clients to listen passively to tapes of their counselling sessions than not to learn anything from counselling sessions.

Key point

Encourage your clients to record and review their counselling sessions since doing so often facilitates their learning of rational concepts. Think about what you particularly want your client to gain from reviewing the tape and instruct him accordingly. Be aware that this method does have its drawbacks and in such instances you need to think carefully about whether the continued use of this method is in a given client's long-term interests.

---

24   Understand the value of self-help forms and teach your clients how to use them

REBC counsellors have developed a number of self-help forms to assist clients in the REBC counselling process. There are forms on which clients write down their problems and related goals, the ABCDE of specific emotional episodes and their homework assignments, amongst others. Throughout this point we will concentrate on forms which clients can use to identify, challenge and change their irrational beliefs. As I (W.D.) have pointed out elsewhere, these forms serve a number of purposes (Dryden, 1994b).

The purposes of ABCDE self-help forms

1   They help your client to organize his experiences in a meaningful way. As such, they offer your client the opportunity to gain a sense of control and counter his tendency to be overwhelmed by his experiences. This is particularly true if your client uses written self-help forms as soon as he begins to feel disturbed.
2   They remind your client that he is expected to help himself, that the effects of therapy do not solely come from attending therapy sessions and that there is much he can do to help himself between sessions.
3   They remind your client about the nature of his problems, the kinds of factors that are relevant in maintaining these problems and what he can do in order to tackle them.

The main features of ABCDE self-help forms

There are a number of such forms in use and frequently REBC counsellors create their own. However, these forms have a number of common features.

1 They make use of the ABC framework for which REBC is well known. As we pointed out in the Introduction, 'A' stands for an activating event (which can be actual or inferential; external or internal and past, present and future – see point 8), 'B' stands for the client's beliefs about A, and 'C' stands for the consequences, the client's unhealthy negative emotions and self-defeating behaviour. These forms are structured in such a way that clients have to put their experiences into the ABC format.

2 They ask clients to dispute their irrational beliefs ('D'). Some forms in fact have two spaces here: one in which clients write down disputing questions and one in which they write down their answers to these questions. These answers should contain the client's new rational beliefs.

3 They contain spaces in which clients write down the emotional and behavioural effects of their new rational beliefs ('E').

In addition, some forms contain a space for clients to write down action-oriented homework assignments which they can do to practise strengthening their rational beliefs.

Training clients to use ABCDE self-help forms

Since ABCDE forms are essentially self-help forms, your client will be expected to complete them between sessions. Thus, their completion constitutes a homework assignment. As such you need to consider the issues that we mentioned in point 22. We will highlight one of those issues here since it is particularly apposite: ensure that your client has the necessary skills to complete the relevant ABCDE form between sessions. To help your client to develop these necessary skills, you need to train him to use the form in the counselling session. In order to do this properly, we suggest you take the following steps.

1 Take your client through a model form.

We suggest that you develop a model ABCDE form for use with clients. In doing so, take your client step-by-step through the form and the responses on it. Since you are not focusing on your client's problem at this time, he is likely to be in the right frame of mind to understand how to use the form. At this stage you may wish to take the client through the model form from start to finish before you answer his questions or you may wish to take and answer questions as you go.

2   Take the client through the form where the focus is on an example of his target problem.

Once your client has understood how to use the form from seeing how it can be applied in 'model' circumstances, ask him to give you a concrete example of his target problem and take him through the form showing him how to fit his experience to the structure of the form. In particular, ask him to select a recent experience which is fresh in his mind since this will help him to understand the form better.

We also recommend that you tape record the process and suggest that your client take the form and the tape home with him and review the tape of the session until he can see quite clearly how you used the form to help him (i) to assess his problem (and, in particular, his irrational beliefs); (ii) to formulate questions designed to challenge his irrational beliefs; and (iii) to answer these questions and formulate new rational beliefs. Suggest that while he is listening to the tape and reviewing the form that he note any points that were unclear or with which he disagreed so that you can discuss these in the following session.

If your client finds going through the entire form in this way too much for him, we suggest that you divide the task into two halves, showing him first how to assess his target problem and when he has understood this, showing him how to challenge and change his identified irrational beliefs.

3   Prompt your client as he takes the lead in using the form with another example of his target problem.

After you have answered your client's questions as suggested above, the next step in the training sequence involves your client taking the lead and using the form with another specific (and preferably memorable) example of his target problem. Your role in this step is to prompt your client when he gets stuck or makes errors in the form's use.

4   Ask your client to complete another ABCDE form on his own in the session and go over it with him when he has completed it.

Your client should now be ready to complete a form on his own. However, since he will require immediate feedback, we suggest that you give him an opportunity to complete a form on a recent example of his target problem during the session so that you can go over it with him. It might be a good idea for you to leave the office at this point to enable your client to complete the form on his own. After 15 minutes you can return and give feedback on what he has done. Do not forget to praise his effort and achievement.

5 Ask your client to complete a number of forms as a homework assignment

Having had the experience of completing the form on his own and getting immediate feedback, your client is probably ready to complete several forms between counselling sessions and receive your delayed feedback a week later. Since ABCDE forms are in general difficult to complete, it is worthwhile stressing to your client that it will take him time to be competent at this task. Do not forget to check all his completed forms, giving precise feedback on each, once again praising both effort and achievement.

6 Suggest that your client complete a form once a day until he can do it in his head.

At this stage, I (W.D.) normally suggest that my client complete an ABCDE form daily until he has developed sufficient expertise to do the exercise (or a suitably shortened version) in his head. I jokingly say at this point: 'An ABC a day, keeps Dryden at bay!' It is important for you to stress to your client that he does not have to wait until he is distressed to use an ABCDE form. He can use it in advance of a possibly disturbing experience or he can use it on past experiences that he found disturbing. He can even do it *during* an emotional episode, even if this means leaving the situation temporarily to complete the form in a private place. If your client complains that he cannot find privacy, suggest that he go to the toilet to complete it there!

In addition, the more your client can complete ABCDE forms with force and energy (particularly the 'D' and 'E' sections), the more benefit he will derive from filling them in.

> **Key point**
>
> There are a number of self-help forms in existence that your clients can use between counselling sessions. Acquaint yourself with them and understand their value. Systematically train your clients in their use, breaking the task down into manageable chunks.

25   Teach your clients how to benefit from using REBC with others

When your clients attempt to teach REBC methods and principles to significant others, they will often increase their *own* facility in applying REBC to their own problems. Bard (1973) has termed this method *rational proselytizing*. In the process of teaching REBC's tenets to other individuals, clients learn to counter their objections and become better able to 'think on their feet' when dealing with their own irrational beliefs. Rational proselytizing can, in fact, be a powerful means for helping many clients to move from *intellectual* to *emotional* insight. Clients can be said to have attained intellectual insight in REBC when they are able to see, with relatively weak and occasional conviction, that a particular irrational belief is false and a corresponding rational belief is true. Emotional insight, which is more likely to lead to significant emotional and behavioural change, is attained when a client has a strong and frequent conviction that an irrational belief is false and a rational belief is true (Dryden and Yankura, 1993; Ellis, 1979c).

While the present point will focus on using rational proselytizing in individual counselling, it is noted that it also has applicability in REBC group counselling. In the group counselling context, clients practise applying REBC concepts and techniques to each others' problems. Ellis (in press) actively encourages his group clients to use REBC with each other in the groups he runs at the Institute for Rational-Emotive Therapy in New York City, and has indicated that he views this method as a particularly powerful tool for fostering therapeutic change.

In the following sections, we review some guidelines for using rational proselytizing with your clients.

Suggest rational proselytizing as a homework assignment

If you vaguely make reference to the potential benefits of rational proselytizing with your client, she may not be too likely to attempt using this technique between counselling sessions. If, however, you specifically suggest it to her as a homework assignment, you will increase the likelihood that she will try it. When you suggest rational proselytizing as a homework assignment, keep the following points in mind.

1 Provide your client with a rationale for engaging in rational proselytizing. Be sure your client understands its major purpose, that is, that it will help her to move from intellectual to emotional insight.

2 Attempt to work with your client to identify particular individuals with whom she can try rational proselytizing. Remember, homework compliance can be increased by specifically identifying the when, where and how of homework enactment. In an ideal scenario, your client will be able to identify a 'target' individual who has a problem similar to her own. Note, however, that your client can also benefit from using rational proselytizing with a person who has a different sort of problem.

3 Be sure to follow up on your client's efforts to engage in rational proselytizing. Check on how your client implemented this homework assignment, just as you would with any other homework assignment that your client takes on. In discussing your client's attempts at rational proselytizing, ask her: (a) with whom she attempted this technique, (b) what problem she 'targeted' with this individual and (c) how successful she thinks she was in applying rational proselytizing to this other person's problem.

4 If your client reports that she experienced difficulties in her deployment of REBC concepts and techniques, discuss these difficulties with her. In particular, help her to refine and strengthen her arguments against irrational beliefs and in favour of rational beliefs.

Some cautions about using rational proselytizing

When you believe that a particular client may benefit from rational proselytizing and are considering suggesting this technique as a homework assignment, bear the following cautions in mind.

Rational proselytizing is best used after your client has attained intellectual insight, and is in the process of working toward emotional insight. Suggesting rational proselytizing to a client who does not yet see that her irrational belief is false makes no clinical sense, and may even be counterproductive in so far as it sets the client up for failure.

Secondly, caution your client against attempting rational proselytizing with an unwilling recipient. Other people will sometimes take offence when someone tries to 'play counsellor' with them. Even if your client is unable to find anyone willing to receive her help with REBC methods, you can still encourage her to try to do ABC analyses (in her own mind) of the upsets she observes other people experiencing. Suggest that she attempt to identify the irrational belief that underpins their upset, and that she practise disputing arguments and rational thinking that would be helpful for countering this particular hypothesized belief.

Thirdly, prepare your client to expect difficulties as she attempts to engage in rational proselytizing. As a counsellor, you can probably recall instances when you did not have a ready response to a given client's objections to your rational arguments. Certainly, your client will encounter pitfalls as she attempts to help other individuals see that their irrational beliefs are false and unhelpful. Present these pitfalls to your client as an almost inevitable part of her learning process. Be sure she understands that any difficulties she encounters in using REBC with others will be discussed when she returns for her next session, and that such discussion will help her to grow in her knowledge and utilization of REBC.

Key point

Suggest rational proselytizing (Bard, 1973) to your clients as a specific homework assignment, and follow up on this as you would with any other homework assignment. Caution your clients against using this technique with unwilling recipients.

---

26 Review homework assignments

Homework is a very important part of REBC. Indeed, research into cognitive behaviour therapy (CBT) has shown that clients who do their homework are more likely to benefit from this approach to counselling than clients who do not (see, for example, Burns and Nolen-Hoeksema, 1991). In addition, it has been shown that clients who terminated CBT prematurely were less likely to do homework than clients who remained in counselling. We have outlined 10 ways in which you can improve the chances that your clients will carry out their homework assignments (see point 22). These tips concerned improvements you can make in negotiating homework assignments with your clients and as such refer to what you can do *before* your clients carry out the assignment.

The importance of reviewing homework assignments

Another way that you can improve the chances that your clients will do their homework is by ensuring that you review it regularly at the beginning of the following session. If you do this you communicate to your clients that you take homework assignments seriously and therefore, in our experience, they are more likely to carry them out. However, if you consistently forget to review homework assignments or if you do so sporadically then, no matter what you *say* about the importance of homework assignments, by your *actions* you communicate that they are of peripheral importance. Consequently, we would hypothesize that clients whose counsellors routinely review their homework assignments are more likely to carry them out than clients whose counsellors do not routinely review these assignments. However, this awaits empirical inquiry. Having provided a rationale for reviewing homework assignments, let us make several suggestions concerning this review process.

Keep a note of your client's homework assignment

You may remember to review your client's homework assignment, but will you remember exactly what he agreed to do for homework? Unless you have an exceptionally good memory, we suggest that you write it down in a form that is easily retrievable when you come to review it. (You can also suggest that your client keep a written record of his assignment to help him in doing it.) On your written note of the client's assignment you can write what your client agreed to do, where and how frequently. Have the client's 'homework record' in front of you at the beginning of every session.

Use encouragement and praise

As most of us know, personal change is a difficult and often uncomfortable process. Since homework is such a central part of this process in REBC, we argue that it is important to be liberal with your praise and encouragement. We are aware that REBC counsellors are often wary of praising and encouraging their clients' efforts and achievements in counselling. In our view, this is due to Albert Ellis's (1982) views of the dangers of counsellor warmth and reinforcement. Ellis is concerned lest such inter-personal qualities lead to the unwitting reinforcement of clients' approval and comfort needs. We concur that this is a risk and needs close monitoring, but if both counsellor and client are clear that by valuing the client's effort and achievements the counsellor is not valuing the client more, this risk can be minimized. Our view is that clients are more likely to continue to do their homework assignments when their efforts and achievements are acknowledged and appreciated than when they are met with a 'matter of fact' counsellor response. Praise and encouragement can be communicated from a position of unconditional acceptance and need not reinforce clients' irrationalities.

Review the homework assignment at the beginning of the next session

Unless there is a good reason for not doing so, we suggest that you review your client's homework assignment with him at the beginning of the next session. Exceptions to this rule concern the need to deal with emergencies and to avoid damaging the therapeutic alliance.

Reviewing the homework at the beginning of a counselling session communicates several things to your client. First, as noted above, it shows that you consider the completion of homework assignments to be a very important component of counselling. Secondly, it shows that homework is an important sustaining link in the process of counselling. By negotiating homework assignments regularly at the end of counselling sessions and by reviewing them routinely at the beginning of subsequent sessions you communicate a counselling pattern that is characterized by the following sequence (DiGiuseppe, personal communication):

Review homework
Do session work
Negotiate homework

This suggests that reviewing a homework assignment should have some impact on the content of the ensuing session and we certainly recommend that this should happen if at all possible. In this way, counselling proceeds in an orderly fashion for clients.

What to do when your client says that he has completed the assignment successfully

When your client says that he has carried out the homework assignment successfully, it is important that you check carefully that he has actually done the assignment as agreed. It is very easy for clients to change the nature of their assignments, often in subtle ways, and therefore careful reviewing is called for. If you find any deviation from the agreed assignment, you need to explore gently the reasons for the modification. In particular, you should note instances where your client changed the nature of the assignment in order to avoid feeling disturbed. If this happens, you should praise your client's efforts, but identify and dispute the irrational beliefs that led to the homework modification. Whenever possible suggest that your client do the assignment again as originally negotiated.

The purpose of many homework assignments in REBC is to facilitate what is called philosophic change (that is, where the client changes his irrational beliefs to their rational alternatives). When you check homework assignments that your client claims to have carried out successfully, you need to evaluate carefully what your client learned. If his learning is based on philosophic change, encourage him to capitalize on his success and negotiate assignments that enable him to consolidate and extend his philosophically based change.

However, if his learning is based on other types of change (as reviewed in point 14), then you need to explain this and negotiate a similar assignment designed to facilitate philosophic change.

What to do when your client's attempt to do the homework assignment 'fails'

We distinguish here between the situation where your client attempts the assignment but is not successful and the situation where he has not even attempted to do it. In this point we will deal with the former and will consider the latter in point 27.

When your client's attempt to do the homework 'fails', first reinforce his attempt and remind him of the no lose concept of homework assignments discussed in point 22. Then, explore with your client the reasons for the attempt not working out. If you find that this situation can be attributed to your failure to suggest a feasible homework assignment, take responsibility for this and say so. In doing so you demonstrate to your client that it is possible to take responsibility for one's errors from a position of self-acceptance.

If, however, your client is largely responsible for the 'failure', encourage him to accept himself as a fallible human being who will fail at times, help him to discover the precise reason for the 'failure', employ problem-solving methods and encourage him to take corrective action, if possible, on the same or similar homework assignment.

Key point

By routinely reviewing your clients' homework assignments, you stress that these assignments are a central part of the change process in REBC. In reviewing assignments, encourage your clients to build on their successes and learn from their 'failures'.

---

27 Identify and deal with reasons for your clients' not attempting negotiated homework assignments

When a client occasionally does not attempt a negotiated home-work assignment, you should treat this seriously and investigate the reasons for this situation. Responding promptly and positively when a client first reports not attempting a homework assignment can help prevent the development of a situation where your client routinely does not attempt negotiated home-work assignments. Unfortunately, some clients will stubbornly refuse to do homework assignments no matter what steps you take to try to encourage them to do so. When this is the case you need to accept this grim reality and help them the best you can without using such assignments.

Fortunately, it is only a minority of clients who steadfastly refuse to do homework assignments throughout counselling. In this point, we will concentrate on helping the majority of clients who eventually will attempt homework assignments, but do not presently do so even though they have agreed to do them. In another publication, I (W.D.) presented a list of reasons that clients have given for not doing their homework assignments and we suggest that you use this list as a guide for identifying why a client did not do an assignment as agreed (Dryden, 1990). You can also give your client this list to complete since it was designed to be used in this way.

Thus, rather than consider again the possible reasons why your client has not attempted a homework assignment, we will outline a number of guidelines for responding to this situation.

Demonstrate full acceptance of your client

While exploring the reasons why a given client did not attempt her homework assignment, it is important that you fully accept your client as a fallible human being, no matter how flimsy her excuse for not doing it or how dismissive she is of your emphasis on the importance of homework assignments. You may legitimately find her behaviour frustrating or annoying, but you need to remind yourself strongly that there is no reason why she must attempt her homework or why she must not be scornful of your efforts. Remember that she is a fallible human being with problems and it is likely that she may demonstrate these problems in her relationship with you, in this case over the issue of homework. It is also helpful if you ask yourself why you must only have clients who are hardworking and devoted to self-help. That would be nice, but is it a necessity? Obviously not! Tell yourself this when you recognize that you are making yourself angry about your client's behaviour.

If you are able to communicate this attitude of non-demanding acceptance to your client and maintain this throughout counselling, then your client may eventually see that it is an attitude worth cultivating towards herself and she may (we stress 'may') start working towards acquiring it. Accepting your clients as fallible, self-defeating human beings may only sometimes encourage your clients to start doing homework assignments, but it is more useful than condemning them.

Remind your client of the no lose concept of homework assignments

No matter how many times your client refuses to do agreed homework assignments, we recommend that you proceed according to the no lose concept of homework assignments (see point 22).

One of my (W.D.) clients stubbornly refused to do any of the assignments we negotiated for several months. At every session, I told her that her refusal to attempt the assignment provided valuable information about blocks to achieving her therapeutic goals. Every week, we identified the same block: a childish wish that I would do the work for her and every week I helped her to see that this would not happen. Then, after the third month of counselling, she started doing her homework assignments. In answer to my inquiry about what had changed, she said: 'I finally saw that you weren't going to help me and that I was going to have to help myself. I gave in before you did!'

We have found that when you persist with this strategy, sometimes your clients will start helping themselves. It is as if the repetition leads to something 'clicking into place' in the client's mind, as demonstrated in the above example.

Take a process view of the non-attempt

Another way of proceeding when your client does not attempt a negotiated homework assignment is to treat the negotiation as the beginning of a process and to track the process until you help your client to find the moment she decided not to do it. Here is an example.

Counsellor: When you agreed to complete the ABC form once a day, did you think that it was a good idea?
Client: At the time, yes.
Counsellor: And did you think that you would do it?
Client: Again, at the time, I did.
Counsellor: When did you begin to change your mind?
Client: I'm not sure.
Counsellor: Well, that night had anything changed?
Client: No.
Counsellor: What about the next morning?
Client: I still intended to do it.
Counsellor: So it was sometime the next day that you decided not to do it?
Client: Yes. I remember that I kept promising myself that I would do it soon, but when 7 pm came I decided not to do it. And then since I hadn't done it the first day, I thought that I'd blown it so I decided not to do it at all.
[*The counsellor noted this and resolved to tackle this idea of 'blowing it' later.*]
Counsellor: What do you think would have made a difference on that first day?
Client: Doing it by noon.
Counsellor: What could you have told yourself to do it by noon? . . .

Here the counsellor tracks the passage of time and helps the client to identify a time when she could have intervened differently with herself to encourage herself to do the assignment. By using this approach, the counsellor does not overdramatize the non-attempt. Rather he shows the client that the difference between doing an assignment and not doing it may be quite small – a point which the client has probably not considered. Also, in using this approach, the counsellor shows the client that if she does something early, she may continue to do it. Normally, the client postpones doing the assignment and continues to postpone doing it. She has thus established for herself a 'not-doing' set. If you can encourage the client to do something to help herself, no matter how small, as early as possible, she may just do it and establish for herself a 'doing' set.

Encourage your client to do *something* to help herself

As noted above, if you can encourage your client to do *something* to help herself, you may help to break her developing habit of not attempting homework assignments. In doing so, you may well have to make significant compromises with your therapeutic ideals. We are referring here to clients who, in general, will probably not achieve any degree of philosophic change. With such clients, you need to set your sights really low and negotiate an assignment that your client will definitely do, even if it means that you are present while she does it. Again your goal is to encourage your client to do *something* to help herself until she has established a 'doing' set. Having helped her to do so, you may later try to encourage her to do something more ambitious.

Be persistent

It is important to be persistent with clients who do not attempt homework assignments. Apart from suggesting a brief break from homework assignments for therapeutic purposes, do not stop asking your clients what they are prepared to do for homework even if they have not attempted an assignment for weeks. You may be tempted to drop the issue under these circumstances, but resist this temptation. Show your clients that you have high frustration tolerance and you may eventually get through to them.

Some years ago, a colleague asked me (W.D.) to see one of his clients with whom he was stuck. I agreed to see her and made tape recordings of the sessions which, with the client's agreement, my colleague listened to. At the end of counselling, from which the client derived moderate gains, my colleague said something which I have not forgotten. He said: 'You didn't do anything different from me, but you persisted a lot longer than I did.'

Learn this lesson and do not give up with clients who do not attempt negotiated homework assignments. Keep showing them that they could live more productive lives if they helped themselves. Keep stressing to clients that they could do the assignments if they chose to. Keep encouraging them, but do not give up on them.

Key point

When working with clients who do not attempt negotiated homework assignments, it is important to demonstrate a number of qualities as you strive to find and address the reasons for their non-attempts. Accept them fully as fallible human beings with a better than average talent for self-defeat, show them there is something to be learned from their refusal to carry out self-help assignments and get them to do something to help themselves no matter how small and seemingly insignificant. Above all, keep persisting and showing them that you will not give up on them even though they tend to give up on themselves.

IV   Enhancing Your Personal and Professional Skills

28 Identify and deal with your own irrational beliefs about your clients and the process of counselling

Even though you are developing your skills as an REBC counsellor, there will still be times when you will tend to think irrationally about your clients and the process of REBC counselling. Remember that, first and foremost, you are human, and as such, in all probability, you will never be immune from irrationalities in either your professional life or your personal life. The best that you can do is to commit yourself to identifying, challenging and changing the irrational beliefs that underpin your unhealthy negative emotions and self-defeating behaviours (including your avoidances and denials).

Albert Ellis (1983) has written a seminal paper on the irrationalities that counsellors bring to their work with clients and hence we will not go over the same ground here. We do, however, recommend that you consult this paper. In this point, then, we will deal with two types of irrationalities that you may have by dint of being a counsellor in general and an REBC counsellor in particular.

Irrationalities related to being a counsellor

Becoming a counsellor does not, as some trainees seem to think, confer upon you certain magical powers. It is to be hoped that you are a reasonably perceptive individual who has a genuine desire to help people help themselves and lead more resourceful and fulfilling lives. If not, a visit to your nearest career counsellor should be a priority. Training and supervision can only help you to develop your helping qualities; it cannot help you to read minds or have infallible intuition. In short, counsellor education cannot stop you from making blunders and some of these will be more serious than you would wish. Consequently, strive to give up demands that you must be right in your assessment or that your interventions must be on target because you are now a counsellor.

Part of counsellor education involves you participating in some form of personal development. Many counsellors appreciate this aspect of their training and say that they benefit enormously from personal work. Nevertheless, no matter how effective your personal work has been you will still disturb yourself; let us hope not as frequently, intensely or for as long as you used to, but disturb yourself you undoubtedly will. Why? Not because you have not been fully analysed, 'gestaltized' or 'rationalized', but because you are a human being. If you accept this reality you will not add to your woes by demanding that you must not be anxious, depressed or whatever because you are now this super being known as a counsellor.

Irrationalities related specifically to being an REBC counsellor

In our opinion, one of the most attractive aspects of REBC is that it is quite precise about a number of important clinical phenomena. Thus, it clearly outlines the type of beliefs that underpin disturbed psychological responses to negative activating events and the type of beliefs that are at the core of healthy responses to these same events. Related to this point, REBC clearly differentiates between unhealthy negative emotions (anxiety, depression, guilt, anger etc.) and healthy negative emotions (concern, sadness, remorse, annoyance etc.).

Thus, as an REBC counsellor, you are given a clear set of guidelines concerning your own psychological functioning when counselling (and in the rest of your life, as we shall see in point 30). Let us articulate this REBC credo as it relates to you in your role as REBC counsellor:

> Strive to minimize your demandingness and awfulizing as this relates to your clients and the counselling process, develop high frustration tolerance about the frustrations of counselling and accept yourself and your clients as fallible human beings.

Now as something to strive for, we think that this credo is really quite clear and if trainees can be rational as they strive to reach this ideal (which cannot be reached as a once-and-for-all, never-to-be-lost state) then this is fine. The problem is that beginning and experienced REBC counsellors alike tend at times to make this professional credo a professional dogma. For example, if you believe that you must not make demands of your clients, you may do one of two things if you recognize that you are in fact making demands on them.

Disturbing yourself about your counselling-related irrationalities and what to do about it

First, you may own up to your demandingness and demand that you must not make demands of your clients. You can even become what Albert Ellis calls a 'talented screwball' by demand-ing that you must not make demands about your original demands. This may seem bizarre, but this is precisely the emotionally disturbed knots that some REBC counsellors get themselves into when they do not adopt a rational philosophy about their own REBC-related irrationalities.

Similar problems emerge when REBC counsellors adopt an irrational perspective on the types of feelings they experience in counselling. For example, knowing that anger is an unhealthy negative emotion to experience about a client one of my (W.D.) trainees became angry at herself for being angry at her client because she believed: 'I must not become angry towards my clients and I am bad for doing so.' She then (as so many trainees do) proceeded to say: 'Oh my God, I'm putting myself down. I really must not do this to myself!'

As trainers we address this issue early on in training and encourage our trainees to develop a healthy philosophy about their irrationalities before encouraging them to adopt the rational credo and look for and work on their primary irrationalities about their clients and the process of REBC counselling.

Denying the problem and what to do about it

The second and more serious thing that you can do when you hold a dogmatic philosophy about being a healthily functioning REBC counsellor is that you can deny that you have a problem. We say that this is more serious because if you deny that you have a problem, you will not work at it, whereas in the first scenario you do at least admit the problem and thus work on it.

The best thing that you can do when you are 'in denial' is to listen to the feedback of others and observe the reactions of your clients. Thus, if several people whom you respect give you feedback that you seem to be getting angry at your clients, for example, accept this at least as a possibility and then ask yourself the following question: 'If I did acknowledge to myself that I have been making myself angry at my clients, how would I honestly feel about that?' If the answer is an unhealthy negative emotion, then the chances are that you have been denying your anger. In this case, assume that you have been angry, accept yourself for your angry feelings and then proceed to look for the irrational beliefs that led to your anger in the first place.

Also, if a number of your clients are getting angry with you, seem increasingly frightened of you or are holding back, then these reactions may well indicate that they are reacting to something unhealthy that is going on in your interactions with them. Acknowledge this possibility, go through the process that we outlined in the previous paragraph and seek supervisory help on the issue. Playing your tapes to your supervisor will be particularly helpful here.

Whether you actively disturb yourself about your counselling-related irrationalities or whether you deny that there is a problem, you do need to help yourself and/or seek help from an REBC counsellor whom you know and trust. You could also set up a self-help group of like-minded REBC practitioners. Guard against believing that because you are an REBC counsellor you must be thoroughly rational!

Key point

Since you are not perfect, it is likely that at times you will bring irrational beliefs to the work you are doing with your clients. Guard against demanding that since you are an REBC counsellor, you must be rational at all times about your clients and the process of counselling. Then, work steadily towards identifying, challenging and changing your initial irrational beliefs. However hard you try, though, it is highly unlikely that you will become perfectly rational about your clients and the process of counselling. Accept this grim reality!

29   Seek regular supervision

Once you have received your basic training in REBC and have started to see clients, it is essential that you receive regular supervision on your practical work if you are to offer a professional service to your clients. Indeed, we believe that seeking regular supervision of your client work over the course of your career is a defining characteristic of professional practice. In this point, then, we will discuss core elements of REBC supervision and focus on how supervision may be conducted.

Supervision of your casework can take place in many formats and utilize different media. There are also the issues of who should serve as an REBC supervisor and how frequently you should be supervised. Let us briefly consider each of these in turn.

The format of supervision

The most common supervisory format involves face-to-face interaction between supervisor and supervisee. This may occur in individual supervision or in a group format. If you are a beginning REBC counsellor we suggest that you have face-to-face individual or small group supervision. At this stage you need the kind of intense individual attention that is suited to your beginning status.

Later on, when you are more experienced, you could benefit more from large group supervision or from non-face-to-face supervision. This latter type of supervision can take place by telephone or more commonly by mail.

Supervisory media

All supervision has an element of case discussion where you and your supervisor discuss salient aspects of a counselling session or case. This medium is especially suited for issues concerning case management or treatment planning.

However, because of the strong emphasis that REBC places on the skills of the counsellor, most REBC supervisors require you to offer audio tapes or video tapes of your work so that they can monitor and give you direct feedback on the skilfullness of your interventions. This is what makes supervision by mail a possibility and enables British REBC counsellors to be supervised by experienced North American supervisors. This form of supervision is not best suited to beginning REBC counsellors since there is little scope for ongoing dialogue. However, as you develop your REBC counselling skills it is useful to get feedback from a variety of supervisors and this is the time to make use of this type of supervision. However, guard against seeking supervision from too many people since you may get confused. Variety can be the spice of supervisory life at this point in your career, but you will not want to get indigestion!

REBC supervision usually involves a mixture of feedback on tapes and case discussion. When supervision through the mail occurs, your supervisor can only comment on your cases, since discussion in the true sense of the word cannot take place in this medium except with long gaps between each party's comments.

Who should supervise?

Supervision can be hierarchical, offered by peers or you can supervise yourself. We recommend hierarchical supervision (which involves you being supervised by an REBC supervisor with more counselling experience than yourself) until you have obtained a high level of skill and have gained a good deal of experience using REBC. At this time, you may rely more on peer supervision, which involves two or more experienced REBC counsellors supervising one another's work. However, you should still seek occasional supervision from a more experienced REBC practitioner and supervisor on difficult cases.

Self-supervision can be carried out at any time, but should be used only as an adjunct to and not as a replacement for hierarchical or peer supervision. When you are supervising yourself, it is helpful to use a self-supervision framework such as the one suggested by Wessler and Wessler (1980) or Yapp and Dryden (1994).

The frequency of supervision

In order to be accredited as a counsellor by the British Association for Counselling (BAC), you need to demonstrate that you are receiving the equivalent of one hour 15 minutes of supervision per month. This is the amount of time in which you are being *directly* supervised on your cases. Thus, if you are attending hierarchical supervision and there are three other counsellors in the group, then you will have to meet once a month for five hours or twice a month for two and a half hours on each occasion if you are to meet this requirement – assuming, of course, that the supervisory time is divided equally among you all.

We consider this ratio of one hour and 15 minutes direct supervision per month to be adequate for experienced REBC counsellors, but not for beginners. In an ideal world, as a novice REBC counsellor you would receive one hour of supervision per week (where the focus is on *your* casework), but since the world is not ideal, we consider that two hours of face-to-face, hierarchical supervision per month is the minimum for a novice.

Choose your supervisor with care

As a final note on supervision, we suggest that you choose your REBC supervisor with care. Before you decide to commit yourself to working with a supervisor, find out first how she structures supervision and how amenable she is to meeting your preferences as a supervisee. If you are a novice our advice is as follows:

1   Choose a supervisor who will spend a good deal of time listening to your tapes and offering you feedback on your developing skills.
2   Ensure that your supervisor will offer you feedback on your skills of working with *both* specific target problems *and* clients over the course of counselling.
3   Disclose any special clinical interests you have as a trainee and discover whether the supervisor is capable of offering supervision on your work in these areas.
4   Spell out in detail what you hope to gain from supervision and gauge the supervisor's reactions. Do not choose a supervisor who is not going to be responsive to your legitimate preferences on this issue.
5   After discussing mutual expectations, ask yourself whether or

not you will be comfortable enough working with this person as your supervisor. Will she provide you with support as well as challenge you at a level which is useful to you or will she be too challenging for you at this phase of your development as an REBC counsellor? Some supervisors are excellent when they supervise more experienced counsellors, but are not so good when working with beginning REBC practitioners.

6   Finally, for reasons such as the one given above, suggest that you meet the supervisor for an agreed number of sessions to determine whether or not she can be helpful to you. This is a crucial time in your development as an REBC counsellor, so take care in whom you place your trust.

Key point

Receiving good supervision is important at any time in your career as a counsellor, but at a time when you are likely to be struggling to use your developing REBC skills with clients, it is central. So take your time and ensure that you will be receiving the right kind of supervision from a supervisor who is sensitive to the healthy requirements of beginning REBC counsellors. Later, as you become more experienced as an REBC counsellor, you can use the full range of supervisory formats and media on offer.

---

30   Develop your own rational self-care philosophy by celebrating your uniqueness

In point 28 we mentioned the types of irrationalities to which you may be particularly prone, given that you are a counsellor and more specifically an REBC counsellor. In this final point we will broaden the issue to consider how you might develop a rational self-care philosophy, including looking after yourself as a counsellor. In doing so, we will particularly highlight areas that are not generally considered in the REBC literature.

As you know, REBC advocates the principle of unconditional self-acceptance. This generally means that we do not merit a legitimate single global rating because (i) we are very complex organisms and (ii) we are ongoing, ever-changing processes. In our view, one concept that needs greater emphasis within the general principle of unconditional self-acceptance is that of uniqueness. Thus, you can choose to accept yourself for your uniqueness. Indeed, we advocate that you celebrate your uniqueness. By this we mean the following.

Be honest with yourself and identify what you value and enjoy

Challenge any irrational beliefs that you spot in your thinking where you demand that since you are an REBC counsellor you must value 'x' or you must be interested in 'y'. Also watch for broader, shame-based irrationalities such as 'Because I am a mature professional, I shouldn't find cartoons funny'. These shame-based irrationalities are rooted in the idea that you are, somehow, a defective, inadequate person if you are drawn to or interested in certain things and not drawn to or uninterested in others. If you discover such irrationalities in your thinking, first accept yourself for having them and then dispute them as vigorously as you can.

Disclose your unique interests to others

The other element in such shame-based irrationalities concerns your inferences about the reactions of others if you disclose your unique interests. Here you infer that if others discover your 'shameful' secret, they would pour scorn on you or ridicule you which would prove that you are an inadequate person. We hold that these inferences are, in general, distorted because they stem from prior irrationalities. Thus, if you believe that you must not have certain interests, then you are more likely to hold negative inferences about the reactions of others should they discover what these are than if you accept yourself for your interests.

What you need to do here is (i) give up the demand that you must not have the interests that you do, in fact, have; (ii) disclose these interests to others and accept yourself in the face of any negative reactions you receive. The more you do this, the more free you will feel to be yourself and the more you will see the distorted nature of your previously held, shame-based inferences.

Accept yourself for your temperament

REBC acknowledges the work of people like Thomas and Chess (1980) who hold that we all have biologically based temperamental tendencies which have an influence on our lives. Thus, in my (W.D.) view, I have a temperament which has the following elements: I am somewhat 'slow to adjust to change'. I have a tendency to be irritable, particularly when under pressure, but can let that go when I receive a positive response from another person. I am also very persistent. I am able to accept myself as a person who has such a temperament and while I have been able to curtail the excesses of my irritability, for example, I accept the grim reality that I am not going to eradicate this entirely from my personality.

We hold that you will take more care of yourself if you identify your temperamentally based patterns and accept yourself for them. You can certainly work to curb the excesses of these patterns, but if you accept the fact that you will not be able to change the 'pull' of your temperament, you will relax and even celebrate your temperament as being part of your uniqueness.

Recognize that you are not Albert Ellis

The point that we want to make here is that it is not a good idea to emulate Albert Ellis's characteristics unless you share his personality, temperament and ideas about a preferred lifestyle. We stress this point because we have seen many beginning REBC counsellors try to emulate Ellis. They do this for two reasons; first, because they believe that they have to act like him to be good REBC counsellors and secondly, because they confuse his personality with the principles of psychological health.

Let us be clear on both these points. First, you do not have to act like Albert Ellis to be a good REBC counsellor. In order to be competent at REBC you need to follow certain points like the ones we have outlined in this book. Acting like Albert Ellis will not add anything to your competence and may, in fact, detract from it as you will be simultaneously trying to do two things: follow helpful practical guidelines and act like somebody else.

Secondly, Albert Ellis's personality is not synonymous with positive mental health. It is possible to be mentally healthy and have a very different personality from his. So, do not try to make yourself into Albert Ellis or anybody else whom you admire. Accept yourself and be yourself. Indeed, we would argue that striving to be mentally healthy and trying to adopt the style of another person are probably mutually exclusive activities. Furthermore, do not uncritically emulate Albert Ellis's lifestyle. He may put work first in his life and devote a large number of hours to promulgating REBC, but you do not have to do either of these things, unless it is really what you want to do and you have a similar hardy temperament which is conducive to long working days.

Key point

It is important that you develop a self-care rational philosophy in life and at work. We suggest that you can do this by celebrating your uniqueness. Identify, challenge and change the beliefs that you may have which will inhibit you doing this. If you look after yourself in the ways that we have outlined and in other ways, doing so will help you to withstand the rigours and enjoy the pleasures of being an REBC counsellor. In life and in work, live long and prosper!

References

Bard, J.A. (1973) 'Rational proselytizing', *Rational Living*, 12 (1): 2–6.

Beck, A.T., Rush, A.J., Shaw, B.F. and Emery, G. (1979) *Cognitive Therapy of Depression*. New York: Guilford.

Bernard, M.E. and Wolfe, J.L. (eds) (1993) *The RET Resource Book for Practitioners*. New York: Institute for Rational-Emotive Therapy.

Bordin, E.S. (1979) 'The generalizability of the psychoanalytic concept of the working alliance', *Psychotherapy: Theory, Research and Practice*, 16: 252–60.

Burns, D.D. and Nolen-Hoeksema, S. (1991) 'Coping styles, homework assignments and the effectiveness of cognitive-behavioral therapy', *Journal of Consulting and Clinical Psychology*, 59: 305–11.

DiGiuseppe, R. (1991) 'Comprehensive cognitive disputing in rational-emotive therapy', in M. Bernard (ed.), *Using Rational-Emotive Therapy Effectively*. New York: Plenum.

DiGiuseppe, R., Leaf, R. and Linscott, J. (1993) 'The therapeutic relationship in rational-emotive therapy: some preliminary data', *Journal of Rational-Emotive and Cognitive-Behavior Therapy*, 11 (4): 223–33.

Dryden, W. (1986) 'Vivid methods in rational-emotive therapy', in A. Ellis and R. Grieger (eds), *Handbook of Rational-Emotive Therapy*, vol. 2. New York: Springer.

Dryden, W. (ed.) (1989) *Howard Young – Rational Therapist: Seminal Papers on Rational-Emotive Therapy*. Loughton, Essex: Gale Centre Publications.

Dryden, W. (1990) *Rational-Emotive Counselling in Action*. London: Sage.

Dryden, W. (1991) 'Language and meaning in rational-emotive therapy', in W. Dryden (ed.), *Reason and Therapeutic Change*. London: Whurr Publishers.

Dryden, W. (1994a) *Invitation to Rational-Emotive Psychology*. London: Whurr Publishers.

Dryden, W. (1994b) *Progress in Rational Emotive Behaviour Therapy*. London: Whurr Publishers.

Dryden, W. (1995a) *Preparing for Client Change in Rational Emotive Behaviour Therapy*. London: Whurr Publishers.

Dryden, W. (1995b) *Facilitating Client Change in Rational Emotive Behaviour Therapy*. London: Whurr Publishers.

Dryden, W. and Feltham, C. (1994) *Developing the Practice of Counselling*. London: Sage.

Dryden, W. and Gordon, J. (1990) *What is Rational-Emotive Therapy? A Personal and Practical Guide*. Loughton, Essex: Gale Centre Publications.

Dryden, W. and Yankura, J. (1993) *Counselling Individuals: a Rational-Emotive Handbook*, 2nd edn. London: Whurr Publishers.

Ellis, A. (1973) 'My philosophy of psychotherapy', *Journal of Contemporary Psychotherapy*, 6 (1): 13–18 (reprinted, New York: Institute for Rational-Emotive Therapy).

Ellis, A. (1975) *How to Live with a Neurotic: at Home and at Work*, rev. edn. New York: Crown.

Ellis, A. (1977) 'Fun as psychotherapy', *Rational Living*, 12 (1): 2–6.

Ellis, A. (1979a) 'Discomfort anxiety: a new cognitive-behavioral construct. Part 1', *Rational Living*, 14 (2): 3–8.

Ellis, A. (1979b) 'The practice of rational-emotive therapy', in A. Ellis and J.M. Whiteley (eds), *Theoretical and Empirical Foundations of Rational-Emotive Therapy*. Monterey, CA: Brooks/Cole.

Ellis, A. (1979c) 'The issue of force and energy in behavior change', *Journal of Contemporary Psychotherapy*, 10: 83–97.

Ellis, A. (1980a) 'Discomfort anxiety: a new cognitive-behavioral construct. Part 2', *Rational Living*, 15 (1): 25–30.

Ellis, A. (1980b) 'The value of efficiency in psychotherapy', *Psychotherapy: Theory, Research and Practice*, 17 (4): 414–19.

Ellis, A. (1982) 'Intimacy in rational-emotive therapy', in M. Fisher and G. Stricker (eds), *Intimacy*. New York: Plenum.

Ellis, A. (1983) 'How to deal with your most difficult client – you', *Journal of Rational-Emotive Therapy*, 1 (1): 2–8.

Ellis, A. (1984) *How to Maintain and Enhance your Rational-Emotive Therapy Gains*. New York: Institute for Rational-Emotive Therapy.

Ellis, A. (1985) *Overcoming Resistance: Rational-Emotive Therapy with Difficult Clients*. New York: Springer.

Ellis, A. (1991a) 'Using RET effectively: reflections and interview', in M.E. Bernard (ed.), *Using Rational-Emotive Therapy Effectively*. New York: Plenum.

Ellis, A. (1991b) 'The revised ABC's of rational-emotive therapy (RET)', *Journal of Rational-Emotive and Cognitive-Behavior Therapy*, 9 (3): 139–72.

Ellis, A. (1994) *Reason and Emotion in Psychotherapy*, 2nd edn. New York: Birch Lane Press.

Ellis, A. (in press) 'Rational emotive behavior therapy (REBT) and its application to group therapy', in J. Yankura and W. Dryden (eds), *A Rational Emotive Behavior Therapist's Casebook*. New York: Springer.

Golden, W.L. (1983) 'Resistance in cognitive-behaviour therapy', *British Journal of Cognitive Psychotherapy*, 1 (2): 33–42.

Horvath, A.O. and Greenberg, L.S. (eds) (1994) *The Working Alliance: Theory, Research and Practice*. New York: Wiley.

Kuhn, T. (1970) *The Structure of Scientific Revolutions*, 2nd edn. Chicago: University of Chicago Press.

Lazarus, A.A. (1981) *The Practice of Multimodal Therapy*. New York: McGraw-Hill.

Lazarus, A.A. and Fay, A. (1982) 'Resistance or rationalization? A cognitive-behavioral perspective', in P.L. Wachtel (ed.), *Resistance: Psychodynamic and Behavioral Approaches*. New York: Plenum.

Maluccio, A.N. (1979) *Learning from Clients*. New York: Free Press.

Maultsby, M.C., Jr (1984) *Rational Behavior Therapy*. Englewood Cliffs, NJ: Prentice-Hall.

Maultsby, M.C., Jr and Ellis, A. (1974) *Technique for Using Rational-Emotive Imagery*. New York: Institute for Rational-Emotive Therapy.

Thomas, A. and Chess, S. (1980) *The Dynamics of Psychological Development*. New York: Brunner/Mazel.

Walen, S.R., DiGiuseppe, R. and Dryden, W. (1992) *A Practitioner's Guide to Rational-Emotive Therapy*, 2nd edn. New York: Oxford University Press.

Wessler, R.A. and Wessler, R.L. (1980) *The Principles and Practice of Rational-Emotive Therapy*. San Francisco, CA: Jossey-Bass.

Yankura, J. and Dryden, W. (1990) *Doing RET: Albert Ellis in Action*. New York: Springer.

Yapp, R. and Dryden, W. (1994) 'Supervision in REBT: the thirteen step self-supervision inventory', *The Rational Emotive Behaviour Therapist*, 2 (1): 16–24.

Young, J.E. (1994) *Cognitive Therapy for Personality Disorders: A Schema-Focused Approach*. Sarasota, FL: Professional Resource Exchange.

Index

CBT (cognitive behaviour therapy)
    107
change xvii–xxiii, 59–62
    behavioural 61, 73
    checking basis of 72–3
    compromise when philosophic
        unattainable 61–2
    criteria for measuring 72
    distraction from negative event 61,
        73
    effort/discomfort involved xix–xx,
        11, 75, 79
    inferential 59–60
    of negative A's 60–1, 73
    obstacles 78–82
    philosophic 59, 73, 109–10
    process of xvii–xxiii
    reviews of 70–4
    spreading effect of xxii–xxiii
clarification of vague client problems
    16–20
cognitive behaviour therapy 107
commitment to REBC xix–xx, xxi, 11,
    75, 100
common themes indicating core
    irrational beliefs 56–7
confidence building 15
consequences (C's, emotional and/or
        behavioural response to beliefs
        about activating events) xvi
    A–C connection 40
    B–C connection 39, 49
    client's dwelling on 31–2
    and ego/discomfort disturbance
        diagnosis 48
coping
    model of self-disclosing disputing
        style 52–3
    rational coping self-statements
        89–90
creativity in use of REBC 63–7

D *see* disputing
demandingness 50, 53, 120, 121
denial of irrational beliefs 121–2
dependency, client's
    on counsellor 75–6, 87
    on tapes of sessions 99
    see also independence
depth-centredness 55

determinants of psychological problems
    xviii
development, personal 120
didactic disputing style 51–2
DiGiuseppe, Ray 49–53, 65
DiMattia, Dom 65
discomfort
    in changing 11, 79
    see also disturbance (discomfort)
disputing (D) xvi, 49–55
    abstraction level 53, 56
    caveats 53–5
    checking client understanding after
        45
    client's independent 101
    comprehensive 49–55
    groundwork 54
    pace 54
    self-help forms and 101
    styles of argument 51–3
        didactic 51–2
        humorous 52, 54
        metaphorical 52
        self-disclosing 52–3, 54–5
        Socratic 14, 51, 52, 75
    to test new rational philosophy 68
    type of argument (logical, empirical,
        pragmatic) 50–1, 54, 63
    vigorous and evocative 91
distraction from negative event 61, 73
disturbance, psychological xii–xv,
    45–9
    avoidance xiv, 48, 109
    discomfort xiii–xiv, 45–6, 75
        and ego disturbance xv, 47–8,
            48–9
        subtle manifestations 47–8
    ego xii–xiii, 45–6
        and discomfort disturbance xv,
            47–8, 48–9
        subtle manifestations 46–7
dogma, professional 120–2
downing, self/other xi–xii, 46, 62, 74,
    98–9
dress for counselling session 4

effects of disputing (E's) xvi–xvii,
    101
effort, client's investment of xix–xx,
    xxi, 11, 75, 100

independence, client's 41, 42, 57, 68,
    85–8
  homework assignments and 11, 85
  see also self-help
inference chaining 36–8, 49
insight, intellectual and emotional
    xx–xxi, 104
insight-oriented therapies 11
interactionism, psychological xvii,
    88–91
irrationality vii–viii
  see also under beliefs

Kelly, George 6

language
  avoiding reinforcing A–C
      connection 40
  establishing shared 20–3
  formal/informal 4
  popular terms 18–19
  term for 'homework assignments' 93
lapse prevention xxi–xxii
LFT (low frustration tolerance) x–xi,
    xiv, 62, 75, 93
listing of problems 12, 71
literature, REBC 42, 63–4
logical disputing arguments 50, 54, 63

manic state 33
mastery model of self-disclosing
    disputing style 52–3
metaphorical disputing style 52
motivation, achievement 69, 79–80
multimodal approach 88–91
musts vs preferences viii–ix
  and achievement motivation 69,
      79–80
  client applies musts to REBC 77–8
  and psychological disturbance xiii,
      xiv

negative emotions *see under* emotions
negative person-rating 50, 53
negotiation of homework assignments
    33, 85–6, 91–5
non-compliance, client's 48, 75, 93,
    111–15
non-verbal cues 4–5, 43–4

operationalizing vague problems 16–20
others, significant
  client's teaching REBC 104–6
  sabotage of client's efforts 80–1

part-whole error xi–xii
penalties 90
persistence 114–15
personal qualities, counsellor's 5–6,
    126–9
pervasiveness 55
philosophy, new rational 57–8, 67–70,
    85
  self-care 126–9
post-therapy stage xxi–xxii, 42
  relapse prevention xxii
  self-help skills xix
  spreading effect of change
      xxii–xxiii
practice, putting REBC into xx–xxi
pragmatic disputing arguments 51, 54,
    63
preferences *see* musts
problem-solving skills xxii
problems
  checking for new 73
  listing 12, 71
  operationalizing vague 16–20
progress reviews 70–4
proselytizing, rational 104–6
psychiatric referral 33
psychoanalysis 11
psychoeducational materials 42
psychological interactionism xvii,
    88–91
psychopathology, client's 7

rational and irrational vii–viii, 21–2
  see also beliefs; philosophy
rational-emotive imagery (REI) 90–1
recordings
  and developing creativity 64–5
  self-help tapes 42
  of sessions 96–9, 102
  for supervision 96, 122, 124
reflection process 24–7
REI (rational-emotive imagery) 90–1
rejection of REBC by client xx, 11, 79
relapse prevention xxii
relationship, counsellor-client *see* bond